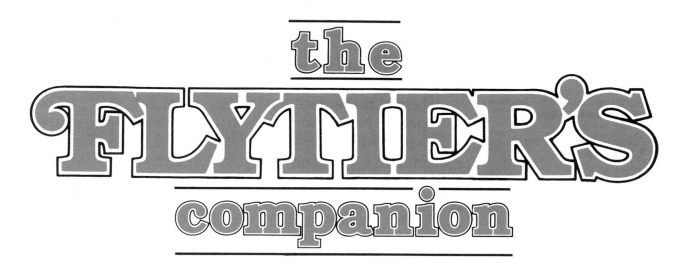

Mike Dawes

Drawings by Taff Price

SWAN·HILL
PRESS

The Flytier's Companion has been edited, designed, and produced by Johnston Co-editions, Box 5054, S-402 22 Gothenburg, Sweden.

Photography: Mike Dawes
Artwork: Taff Price
Design: Lena Gustavsson

Lithography: Repro-Man, Gothenburg
Typesetting: Concept Communications, Crayford, England.

This edition first published in 1989 by Swan Hill Press, an imprint of Airlife Publishing Ltd.

ISBN 1-85310-085-4

British Library Cataloguing in Publication Data available.

Swan Hill Press
An imprint of Airlife Publishing
101 Longden Road, Shrewsbury
SY3 9EB England.

Author's Acknowledgements

With his artistic skill, vast knowledge of entymology, and his proficiency in the art of flytying, Taff Price helped make our first book the great success it is. The present book is our response to appeals from all over the world for a follow-up volume. Once again, Taff has played a vital part in the production. I count myself fortunate to have had his vast experience upon which to draw.

Bev Harper-Smith is a very talented flytier whose flies are works of art and a delight to photograph. He tied some of the best flies in my first book, and I was very pleased when he agreed to tie all of the trout flies in this book. Only a few professional flytiers can ascend to his level, so he sets a standard of excellence at which most of us amateurs can only aim.

When it came to tying the steelhead flies, I was fortunate to find Harry (Tex) Ranger, a highly talented amateur flytier who won both of the 1988 novice's awards, for trout and for salmon flies, awarded by the Fly Dressers Guild. He took up flyfishing and flytying only three years ago, and already his work is of an admirable standard.

Since our first book was published, flytiers all over the world have written to me concerning the exact hooks used in the patterns I described. My company, Graham Trout Flies, has where possible always used Kamasan hooks, as I consider them excellent. Those for whom this brand is not available can find a suitable hook size and type given for each pattern, but those who can obtain Kamasan hooks will find the correct hook designation for each given in the index at the back of the book.

I look forward to receiving readers' reactions to the patterns given here — advice, criticism, and points of view are always welcome.

This book is dedicated to my mother.

Mike Dawes
Graham Trout Flies
Herefordshire HR2 8DG

Contents

Fishing the River Spey in Scotland.

I
NYMPHS

Ardleigh Nymph

This fly is a variation of the Pheasant Tail Nymph. It was created by Richard Connell, and it is reputed to be as successful on Ardleigh reservoir as the Grenadier is at Chew.

Hook: *Down-eyed 10-16*
Thread: *Pre-waxed black*
Tail: *Greenwell hackle fibres*
Body: *Cock Pheasant tail fibres*
Rib: *Fine oval gold tinsel*
Thorax: *Peacock herl*
Hackle: *Greenwell hen (light furnace)*
Head: *Black*

1

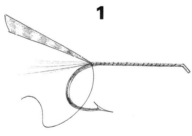

Take the tying thread down the shank to the bend and there tie in the fibres of Greenwell hackle. At the same point, tie in a length of fine oval gold tinsel and the cock Pheasant tail fibres.

2

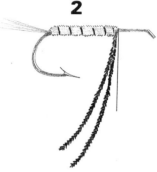

Return the thread two-thirds of the way up the shank, then form the body by following with the cock Pheasant tail fibres. Secure and remove any surplus fibre. Now rib the body with the fine oval gold tinsel. At this point, tie in a couple of strands of Peacock herl.

3

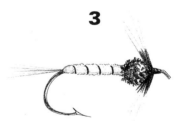

Wind on the Peacock herl to form a round button-like thorax. Tie off and cut away any surplus herl. Finally wind on a collar hackle of Greenwell hen. Finish the fly in the usual way.

August Dun

This pattern was created by Thomas Clegg, a pioneer in the use of fluorescent materials in fly dressing. It was tied to represent the nymph of the August or Autumn Dun *(Ecdyonorus dispar)* and it uses a body of bright-green fluorescent floss.

Hook: *Down-eyed 12-14*
Thread: *Pre-waxed light green*
Tail: *Yellow-dyed Guinea Fowl fibres*
Body: *Signal-green fluorescent floss*
Rib: *Copper wire*
Thorax: *Blue-dun/olive fur (the original used monkey)*
Wingcase: *Squirrel-tail hair*
Legs: *The thorax hair picked out*
Head: *Green*

This is a straightforward nymph pattern. Follow the instructions for the Butcher Nymph (page 13).

Baddow Special

This pattern was created by John Poole and first used on Hanningfield Reservoir in Essex. It is used as a Damsel larva imitation but can also double as a Caddis larva of sorts.

Hook: *Down-eyed 8-12 long shank*
Thread: *Pre-waxed black*
Tail: *Green fluorescent wool*
Body: *Peacock herl*
Rib: *Gold or silver wire*
Hackle: *White cock*
Head: *Black*

1

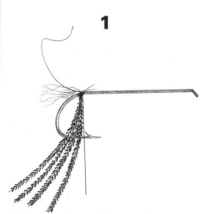

Take the thread down the shank to the bend and tie in a tuft of the green fluorescent wool for the tail. At the same point tie in the gold or silver wire for the rib and about three strands of Peacock herl for the body.

2

Return the thread back up the shank and follow with the Peacock herl. Secure and remove any surplus herl. Wind on the rib, tie off, and remove any surplus material.

3

Wind on a white cock hackle.

This fly can be pre-weighted with lead wire if so desired.

Barrie Welham Nymph

The original name of this fly was the BW Nymph, thus christened because it was tied with brown wool. By coincidence the letters are the same as the originator's initials and over a period of time the fly became known as the Barrie Welham. It is a useful broad-spectrum pattern for both stream and still water and is especially effective during a buzzer rise.

Hook: *Down-eyed 10-12*
Thread: *Pre-waxed black*
Tail: *Fluorescent red and yellow floss silk*
Body: *Brown wool*
Rib: *Fine oval gold tinsel*
Breathing filaments: *White cock-hackle fibres*
Head: *Black*

1

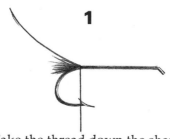

Take the thread down the shank to the bend and tie in a short tuft of the fluorescent red and yellow floss silk. At the same point tie in a length of the fine oval gold tinsel.

2

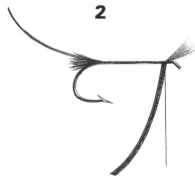

Return the thread up the shank and tie in a length of the brown wool and a tuft of white cock-hackle fibres. (The hackle fibres can be tied in after the body has been wound if you want to allow them to slope back over the back, but if you require them to be a little more realistic, tie the fibres in at this stage. They will subsequently appear to be more like the natural breathing filaments of a Chironomid midge pupa).

3

Wind the wool down the body and back again and follow this with the fine oval gold tinsel. Tie off and trim away any surplus material. Form a small neat head, whip finish, and varnish.

Black Marabou Pupa

Taff Price tied this pattern because he wanted a pupa pattern with a little more integral life. Marabou feather is highly mobile and the slightest twitch on the line pulsates the fly in a most enticing manner.

Hook: *Down-eyed 10-16*
Thread: *Pre-waxed black*
Tail: *Black Marabou*
Body: *Dubbed black Marabou (if a smoother body is desired use floss silk)*
Rib: *Oval silver tinsel*
Thorax: *Bronze Peacock herl*
Breathing filaments: *White cock-hackle fibres*
Head: *Black*

1

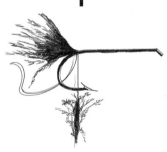

Take the thread down the shank to the bend and tie in a tuft of the black Marabou for the tail, which in essence is an extension of the body. At the same point tie in a length of the oval silver tinsel for the rib. Dub some Marabou feather onto the tying thread.

2

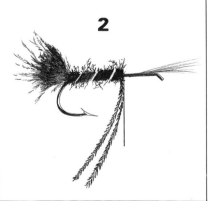

Return the dubbed thread two-thirds of the way up the shank to form the body. Rib the body with the oval silver tinsel. Secure and cut off any surplus. Tie in a few fibres of bronze Peacock herl. On top of the hook tie in a bunch of white cock-hackle fibres so that they project over the eye.

3

Form the thorax with the Peacock herl and secure. Remove any surplus herl. Form a neat head and varnish. Trim the white cock-hackle fibres.

Bloodworm

The larval stage of the Chironomid midge has many imitations. This one, by Roger Fogg, is a simple pattern to tie and represents the species of the larva that has a high haemoglobin factor.

Hook: *Sedge or grub hook 10-12*
Thread: *Pre-waxed red*
Body: *Flat red tinsel (Lurex)*
Rib: *Oval or round red tinsel*
Thorax: *Scarlet seal's fur or substitute*
Head: *Red*

1

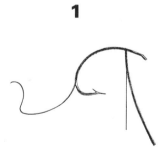

Take the thread down the shank to the point shown and there tie in a length of oval or round red tinsel for the rib. Note that the dressing goes right around the bend of the hook. Return the thread back up the shank and there tie in a length of the flat red tinsel.

2

Form the body by winding the flat red tinsel down the shank and back again. Follow with the rib. Secure and cut off any surplus. Dub the scarlet seal's fur onto the thread.

3

Form the thorax by winding the fur-laden thread around the shank. Finish with a small head, whip finish, and varnish.

Blue Winged Olive Nymph

There are a number of nymphs tied to represent the larval stage of the mayfly known as the Blue Winged Olive *(Ephemerella ignita)*. This particular pattern is an American nymph used to imitate such native species as *Drunella flavilinea* and other *Ephemerella*.

Hook: *Down-eyed 10-16*
Thread: *Pre-waxed olive*
Tail: *Lemon Wood Duck flank fibres*
Body: *Olive seal's fur or substitute*
Rib: *Brown silk*
Thorax: *Olive seal's fur or substitute*
Hackle: *Brown Partridge hackle*
Wingcase: *Grey Goose or Duck wing quill slip*
Head: *Olive*

Follow the instructions for the Water Tiger (page 40) and substitute with the appropriate materials.

Booby Nymph

This pattern was created by Gordon Fraser, the Leicestershire nymph specialist, and is generally used with a sinking line. The buoyancy provided by the polystyrene beads allows the fly to swim above the bottom. When used with a floating line, it can still take its share of trout in the surface film, because it is practically unsinkable. This fly can be tied in a number of different colours. Any type of nymph can be adorned with these polystyrene beads.

Hook: *Down-eyed 8-10 long shank*
Thread: *Pre-waxed orange*
Tail: *Orange Marabou*
Body: *Orange seal's fur or substitute*
Rib: *Gold or silver tinsel*
Head: *Two polystyrene beads*

1

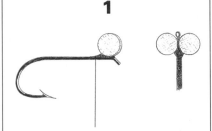

Cut out a small piece of white nylon (stockings or tights) and form a little bag into which the polystyrene beads are placed. Tie the bag at the front of the hook. The two balls are separated by a figure-of-eight whip.

2

Take the thread down the shank to the bend and tie in a bunch of orange Marabou. This gives movement to the fly. At the same place, tie in the ribbing tinsel. Dub the thread with some orange seal's fur.

3

Take the fur-laden thread down the shank to form the body, then follow this with the ribbing tinsel. Secure the rib and finish off the fly behind the polystyrene beads.

Butcher Nymph

This pattern is a nymph-shaped version of the classic wet Butcher. The difference lies in the fact that the wing on the original has been substituted for a wingcase, and a thorax of black fur is added to enhance the nymphal shape. This fly is an attractor pure and simple.

Hook: *Down-eyed 8-14*
Thread: *Pre-waxed black*
Tail: *Scarlet cock-hackle fibres*
Body: *Flat silver tinsel or Lurex*
Rib: *Fine oval silver tinsel*
Thorax: *Black fur*
Wingcase: *Black feather fibre (e.g. Crow)*
Hackle: *Black hen*
Head: *Black*

1

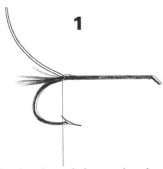

Take the thread down the shank to the bend and tie in a bunch of the scarlet cock-hackle fibres for the tail. At the same place tie in a length of fine oval silver tinsel for the rib.

2

Return the thread up the shank and tie in a length of the flat silver tinsel or Lurex.

3

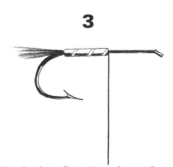

Wind the flat tinsel or Lurex down the shank and back. Tie off. Follow with the oval silver tinsel. Tie this off too, and cut off any surplus.

4

Tie in a slip of Crow feather fibre and dub some black fur onto the tying thread.

5

Form a thorax with the dubbed thread and take the Crow feather fibre back over the back, tie off, and cut off any surplus feather.

6

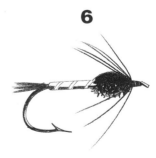

Finally wind on a black hen hackle, whip finish, and varnish.

Caddis Pupa

This particular pattern uses the Swannundaze plastic strip for the body (see Swannundaze Stonefly Larva, page 36). This material is excellent for forming the natural segmentation of an insect's body.

Hook: *Caddis hook*
Thread: *Pre-waxed brown*
Underbody: *Green Mylar or Lurex*
Overbody: *Clear Swannundaze*
Thorax & Legs: *Red squirrel underfur and guard hairs dubbed on and then picked out to simulate legs*
Head: *Brown*

1

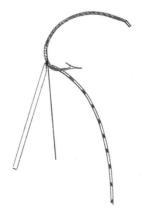

Take the thread down the shank and around the bend of the hook. There tie in a strip of green Mylar or Lurex and a length of clear Swannundaze.

2

Form the abdomen by first returning the thread to the point shown in the drawing and then following with the green underbody material. Tie off and cut away surplus. Now wind the Swannundaze over the underbody. Tie off and remove any surplus. Dub the squirrel fur onto the thread.

3

Wind on the fur-laden thread towards the eye. Finish off the fly in the usual manner, then pick out some of the squirrel-fur fibres to form the legs.

Damsel Wiggle Nymph

This style of jointed fly was popularized by Swisher, Richards and Whitlock in the United States and by John Goddard in Great Britain. The most recent innovation in the design of the jointed fly is a new pattern for hoppers devised by Gary LaFontaine. Even small minnow lures can be easily devised in the same way. The most important characteristic of all these flies is the integral mobility provided by the jointed hook.

Hook: *Ring-eyed 10-12 long shank and down-eyed 8-10*
Thread: *Olive*
Tail: *Olive cock-hackle tips*
Body: *Olive seal's fur or substitute*
Rib: *Fine silver tinsel, flat or oval*
Thorax: *Dark-olive seal's fur or substitute*
Wingcase: *Dyed brown Turkey tail or cock Pheasant centre-tail fibres*
Hackle: *Olive cock*
Head: *Olive*

This fly is tied in two parts: the abdomen and the thoracic part.

1

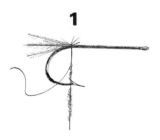

Starting with the long-shank hook, take the thread down the shank to the bend and tie in three cock-hackle tips. At the same point, tie in the ribbing tinsel. Dub the olive seal's fur onto the tying thread.

2

Take the fur-laden thread back down the shank to form the abdomen. Follow with the ribbing tinsel. Finish off with a whip finish and varnish. Shear off the bend portion of the hook. The lower drawing shows the sheared-off hook from above.

3

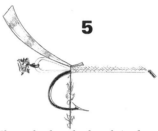

Place the second hook (normal-shanked) in the vice. Take the tying thread down the shank to the bend and tie in a length of jointing material, such as piano wire, monofilament nylon, or Kevlar thread.

4

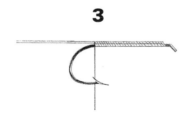

Slip the first hook onto the jointing medium, and whip the end of the medium back over the shank

of the second hook. A coat of adhesive helps to secure.

5

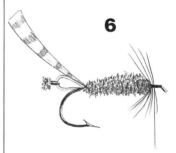

When the hook shank is dry, take the tying thread back down the shank to the bend and tie in a strip of the Turkey feather or cock Pheasant centre-tail for the wingcase. Dub the dark-olive seal's fur onto the tying head.

6

Take the fur-laden thread up the shank to form the thorax, and then tie in an olive cock hackle.

7

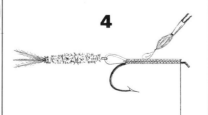

Bring the wingcase feather over the back, secure, and cut off any surplus. Finish the fly in the usual way.

Dark Grey Larva

This American pattern imitates the larval stage of the caddis or sedge family *(Trichoptera)*. There are many patterns in use today to imitate the larva and the pupa forms of these important flies.

Hook: *Down-eyed 10-14*
Thread: *Pre-waxed brown*
Body: *Hare's ear*
Rib: *Fine gold wire*
Hackle: *Brown Partridge*
Thorax: *Dark-brown fur*
Head: *Brown*

1

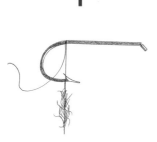

Take the thread down the shank to the bend and tie in a length of the fine gold wire. Dub the fur onto the thread.

2

Take the fur-laden thread up the shank to form the body. Follow this with the fine gold wire. Now tie in a few fibres of brown Partridge beneath the hook to simulate legs.

3

Dub some dark-brown fur onto the tying thread and wind it around the shank to form a thorax. Complete the fly as usual.

Footballer

This imitation of the Chironomid midge pupa was devised by Geoffrey Bucknall. It gets its name from the black-and-white striped effect of the natural creature's abdomen, which looks like a footballer's jersey. The original fly used horsehair as the body medium. More recently, black-and-white monofilament nylon has been used. The fly is usually fished in or just under the surface.

Hook: *Down-eyed 12-16*
Thread: *Pre-waxed black or grey*
Body: *Alternate bands of black and white horsehair*
Thorax: *Mole fur*
Head: *Peacock herl*

1

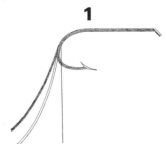

Take the thread down the shank and past the bend as shown. There tie in a length of black and a length of white horsehair.

2

Return the thread back along the shank and follow it with even alternate bands of the horsehair. Secure and cut off any surplus horsehair. Dub a small pinch of mole fur onto the tying thread.

3

Wind on the fur-laden thread to form the thorax and then tie in a strand of Peacock herl.

4

Wind on the herl to form the head and complete the fly in the usual way.

Green Beast

A green version of the Water Tiger, this pattern was devised by Alan Pearson for reservoir rainbows. It is generally tied weighted and fished close to the bottom.

Hook: *Down-eyed 8 long shank*
Thread: *Green*
Tail: *Grass-green cock-hackle fibres*
Body: *Grass-green floss silk*
Rib: *Fine silver wire*
Hackle: *Brown Partridge*
Head: *Green*

1

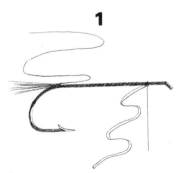

Take the thread down to the bend and tie in the grass-green cock-hackle fibres for the tail. Also tie in the fine silver wire for the rib. Return the thread up the shank and tie in a length of the grass-green floss silk.

2

Form the body by winding the floss silk down the hook and back again. The body should have a nicely tapered shape. When the body is tied, wind on the rib.

3

Strip the fibres from one side of a brown Partridge hackle and tie the hackle in by the tip on top of the hook. Wind the hackle on. Finish the fly in the usual way, with a neat head and a whip finish.

Green Insect

The original Green Insect utilized green Peacock herl for the body. In this modern version green fur dubbing is used. This fly can be used as a wet or a dry pattern. In smaller sizes it is considered to be a favourite pattern for grayling. This version, if weighted, makes a very good nymph pattern for still-water trout.

  Hook: *Down-eyed 10-14*
  Thread: *Pre-waxed black or green*
  Body: *Green seal's fur or substitute*
  Rib: *Fine silver tinsel or wire*
  Hackle: *Blue-dun*
  Head: *Green*

1

Take the thread down the shank to the bend and tie in a length of the tinsel or wire. Dub some green seal's fur or substitute onto the thread.

2

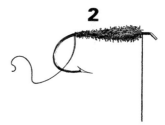

Wind the dubbed thread down the shank to form a carrot-shaped body.

3

Wind on the tinsel or wire. Finally wind on a blue-dun hen or soft cock hackle. (For the dry version use a stiff blue-dun cock hackle).

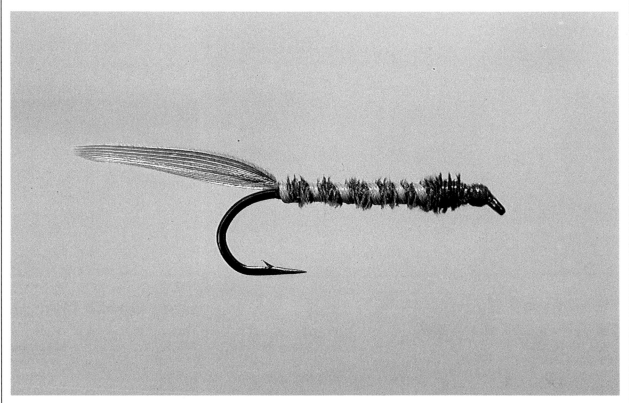

Green Larva

Chironomid larvae live in the mud but leave this sanctuary to replenish their oxygen supply in the more heavily oxygenated levels of the water. It is then that they receive the attention of the trout. This pattern of John Goddard's is a sister pattern to his Red Larva.

Hook: *Down-eyed 8-12 long shank*
Thread: *Pre-waxed olive or green*
Tail: *A strip of dyed olive green Goose feather*
Body: *Olive-dyed feather herl (Condor substitute)*
Rib: *Green fluorescent floss silk*
Thorax: *Buff-coloured feather herl (Condor substitute)*
Head: *Olive*

The Condor is a protected bird, and therefore its feathers are unavailable for fly tying. It is more usual to use a substitute. The normal substitutes sold are dyed Goose quills, which make no difference to the overall appearance of the fly.

1

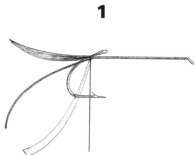

Take the thread down the shank to the bend and there tie in a strip of the dyed olive-green Goose feather for the tail, which must be long and curved to be effective in the water. At the same point tie in a length of olive-dyed feather herl for the body and a length of the green fluorescent floss silk for the rib.

2

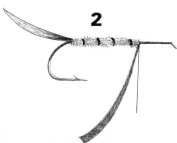

Return the thread back along the shank. Form the body by winding the olive-dyed feather herl up the shank. Follow this with the ribbing silk, tie off, and cut away any surplus. Now tie in a length of the buff-coloured feather.

3

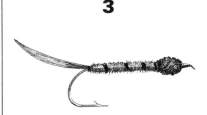

Form a thorax of sorts with the buff herl and tie off. Form a neat head, whip finish, and varnish.

Hatching Midge Pupa (Collyer)

This pattern was devised by Dave Collyer, the well-known Surrey flytier and author of *Fly Dressing One* and *Fly Dressing Two*. It represents the Chirono-mid midge at the surface prior to hatching. See also Goddard's Suspender Buzzer (page 35).

Hook: *Down-eyed 10-14*
Thread: *Pre-waxed olive*
Body: *Fine olive wool, silk, or feather fibre*
Rib: *Fine flat silver tinsel*
Head: *Clipped deer hair*

Other colours are also tied. Just substitute black, red, brown, etc. for the olive.

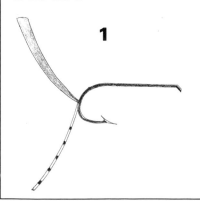

1

Take the thread down the shank and around the bend of the hook. There, tie in a length of fine flat silver tinsel for the rib and a length of the olive body material chosen.

2

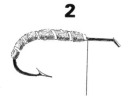

Form the body by returning the thread back along the shank to the point shown and by follow-ing this with the body material and then the fine flat silver tinsel for the rib. Secure and cut away any surplus.

3

Cut off a small bunch of deer body hair and lay it on top of the hook. Take three turns of thread around it and pull tight.

4

The downward pull of the thread causes the hair to flare around the shank. Repeat this process until the shank is full up.

5

Clip the deer hair into a ball shape and then finish the fly in the usual way.

Inchworm

This pattern is an imitation of a caterpillar. The larvae of moths and also of sawflies (*Hymenoptera*) are quite often taken by trout. This is especially true of trout that lie beneath the shade of trees. Many species of larva descend from such tress on a silken strand that they spin for the purpose. If the tree overhangs water, then the grub may well end up as food for trout.

Hook: *Down-eyed 12-16 long shank*
Thread: *Pre-waxed black, yellow, or green*
Body: *Insect-green dyed deer hair*
Rib: *Insect-green floss silk (a darker green can be used to give a more segmented effect)*
Head: *Yellow*

1

Take the thread down the shank and tie in the ribbing silk.

2

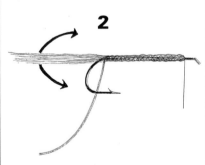

Return the thread back up the shank and tie in at the eye a sparse bunch of the dyed deer hair, which must be twice the length of the shank. Take the thread along the shank and back again, trapping the deer hair the whole length.

3

Pull back the deer hair now projecting out of the back of the hook and tie it in at the head. Now take the ribbing silk in neat even turns up the shank and secure. Trim off any excess hair and silk, form a neat head, and complete the fly with the usual whip finish and varnish.

Ivens' Brown & Green Nymph

Tom Ivens, a pioneer of modern reservoir fishing, created a number of patterns, of which this is one of the most popular. A broad-spectrum nymph pattern, it makes a very good sedge pupa imitation. It is normally tied on short-shank hooks, but occasionally it is very successful tied on a long-shank hook, as depicted here.

Hook: *Down-eyed 8-12 long shank or short shank*
Thread: *Olive*
Tail: *Four strands of Peacock herl*
Body: *One brown and one green Ostrich herl, twisted together*
Rib: *Fine oval gold tinsel*
Back: *Peacock herl*
Hackle: *None*
Head: *Peacock herl*

1

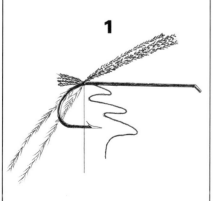

After taking the thread down the hook, tie in the four strands of Peacock herl so that they project as a tail out of the back. The remainder will be used for the back. At the same point tie in a length of fine oval gold tinsel and one strand each of brown and green Ostrich herl.

2

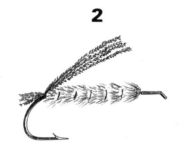

Return the thread back up the shank and follow this with the Ostrich herl, which has been first twisted into a rope to mix the colours. Follow the body with the tinsel in even turns.

3

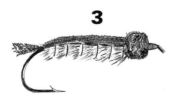

Take the Peacock herl over the back and tie off. Tie in two more strands of Peacock herl, twist into a rope, and form into a neat round head. Whip finish and varnish to complete the fly.

Killer Bug

This simple pattern was devised by the late Frank Sawyer, perhaps one of the greatest exponents of nymph fishing of recent times. He devised this maggot of a fly to take grayling on his beloved Hampshire Avon. The fly was originally tied using Chadwick's No 477, a darning wool of a grey colour but with a distinct pinkish cast.

Hook: *Down-eyed 10-14*
Thread: *Copper wire*
Underbody: *Fine copper wire*
Overbody: *Chadwick's 477 wool or substitute*

1

Form a shape with the copper wire.

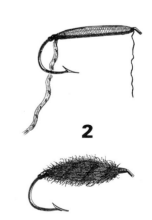

2

Tie in the wool and wrap around. Tie off, whip finish and varnish.

Leadwing Coachman Nymph

First there came the Coachman fly, a white-winged fly normally fished wet. Then the pattern was given a grey wing and became the Leadwing Coachman. Both these wet flies were in turn re-tied as nymphs. This is a favourite pattern of many American fly-fishermen. It is a broad-spectrum nymph, imitating nothing in particular but proving most attractive to the trout.

Hook: *Down-eyed 8-12*
Thread: *Pre-waxed black*
Tail: *Brown cock hackle*
Body: *Bronze Peacock herl*
Hackle: *A few fibres of brown cock hackle tied as a beard*
Wing (wingcases): *Grey Mallard shoulder feather*
Head: *Black*

1

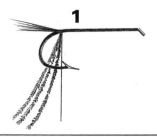

Take the thread down the shank to the bend and tie in the tail, either a single brown hackle point or a few fibres of brown cock hackle. At the same place tie in a few bronze Peacock herls.

2

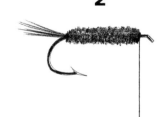

Form a rope with the Peacock herl and the tying thread and wind back up the hook shank to form the body.

3

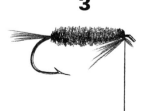

Tie in a few fibres of brown cock hackle beneath the hook.

4

Cut the tip of a grey shoulder feather from a Mallard to the shape shown.

5

Tie the cut feather tip on top of the hook to form a wing pad. Finish the fly in the usual way.

Marabou Damsel Nymph

The larva of the Damsel Fly is a very important item in the diet of the trout, especially in still water. From the month of June until September in Great Britain, the trout will feed avidly upon nymphs and take the slim adults if they land on the surface. This pattern relies on the highly mobile Marabou feather to give integral life to the fly. It is probably one of the best imitations of the natural. It can be tied in olive or in brown.

Hook: *Down-eyed 8-12 long shank*
Thread: *Pre-waxed olive*
Tail: *Olive Marabou*
Body: *Olive Marabou*
Rib: *Copper wire*
Thorax: *Olive Marabou*
Wingcase: *Olive Goose or Swan*
Eyes: *Monofilament nylon (20 lb)*
Head: *Olive*

1

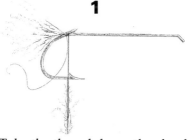

Take the thread down the shank and there tie in a bunch of the olive Marabou for the tail. Also tie in a length of copper wire for the rib. Dub some olive Marabou feather fibre onto the thread.

2

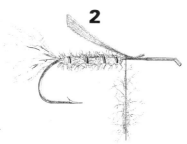

Take the feather-laden thread down the shank to the point shown, thus forming the body. Follow this with the copper-wire rib. Now tie in on top of the hook a slip of olive Goose or Swan feather for the wingcase. Dub a further quantity of olive Marabou onto the tying thread.

3

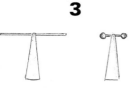

Tale a piece of the monofilament nylon and hold in a pair of tweezers. Apply a naked flame to the ends and melt to form two little balls. These will be the eyes of the fly.

4

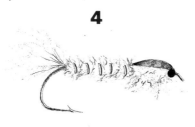

Wind on the dubbed thread to form the thorax and then tie in the nylon "eyes". Take the olive Goose or Swan feather fibre over the back of the thorax and tie off. Remove any surplus feather fibre and form a neat head. Finish the fly in the usual way. Pick out the Marabou around the thorax with a dubbing needle to simulate the legs.

Olive Quill Nymph

Like the Greenwell Nymph this pattern is based on the more usual wet or dry Olive Quill and is used by those who for one reason or another refuse to fish wet flies, preferring patterns that emulate the nymphal stages of the aquatic insects more closely.

Hook: *Down-eyed 12-16*
Thread: *Pre waxed olive or black*
Tail: *Olive hackle fibres*
Body: *Stripped Peacock herl (this can be dyed olive or left undyed)*
Thorax: *Olive seal's fur or substitute*
Hackle: *Olive hen*
Head: *Olive*

1

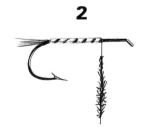

Wind the thread down to the bend of the hook and tie in a few fibres of olive hackle for the tail. Tie in a piece of stripped Peacock herl for the body.

2

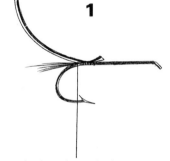

Return the thread two-thirds along the shank. Carefully wind the Peacock herl the same distance up the shank. Tie off and cut away surplus. Dub the olive seal's fur or substitute onto the tying thread for the thorax.

3

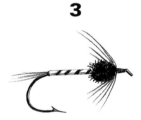

Wind on the thorax and an olive hen hackle and finish the fly in the usual way.

Seal's Fur

Due to conservation measures and the ban imposed on seal products by many countries, the use of the fur in tying flies is a thing of the past. Modern man-made products have now to a great extent supplanted the seal's fur. Polypropylene, Antron, etc are the common substitutes. Throughout the book, however, we give seal's fur in the dressing, so that the original dressing is not lost, but the reader should use an appropriate substitute.

P.V.C. Nymph

One of John Goddard's many effective patterns, this fly can be used to imitate both the Lake Olive *(Cloeon simile)* and the Pond Olive *(Cloeon dipterum)*. It can also be used on rivers for many species of olive-coloured nymphs. The P.V.C. outer skin imitates the natural transparency of the real larva.

Hook: *Down-eyed 10-14*
Thread: *Brown*
Tail: *Olive Condor herl*
  (substitute: olive-dyed Goose)
Underbody: *Copper wire*
Overbody: *Olive-brown*
  Condor herl or substitute
  covered with P.V.C. strip
Thorax: *Same as overbody but*
  not covered by the P.V.C.
Wingcase: *Grey/brown feather*
  fibre
Head: *Olive*

1

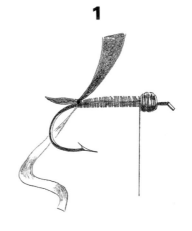

Weight the fly with a copper-wire underbody formed into the shape shown. Take the thread down the shank and tie in the herl or substitute for the overbody and the tail. At the same point tie in a strip of P.V.C. film. Return the thread about two-thirds of the way up the shank.

2

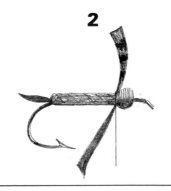

Form the overbody by first winding the herl up the shank. Follow this with the P.V.C. film. Do not cut off the surplus herl, as this is to be used for the thorax, but cut away any surplus film after securing it. At this point tie a strip of grey or brown feather fibre on top of the hook for the wingcase.

3

Form the thorax with the surplus overbody herl and then take the wingcase over it. Secure the wingcase, cut off any surplus and form a neat head. Whip finish and varnish as usual.

Quill Gordon Nymph

Here is another case of a nymph pattern created from a dry fly. The original pattern, namely the Quill Gordon, was created by the father of American dry-fly fishing, Theodore Gordon. It can be used to imitate a wide number of small to medium mayflies, among them *Epeorus pleuralis*. This nymph pattern is also of the broad-spectrum type.

Hook: *Down-eyed 10-14*
Thread: *Pre-waxed brown or olive*
Tail: *Dark cock Pheasant centre tail*
Body: *Fur from a beaver's belly*
Rib: *Brown silk*
Hackle: *Brown Partridge*
Wingcase: *Brown mottled Turkey or similar feather*
Head: *Brown*

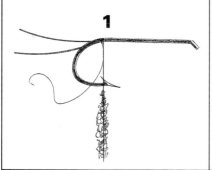

1

Take the thread down the shank to the bend and tie in two strands of dark cock Pheasant centre tail and a length of brown silk for the rib. Dub the tying thread with the beaver fur.

2

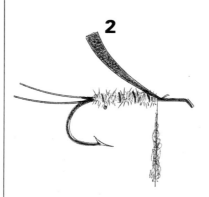

Return the fur-laden thread back along the shank to form the body. Follow this with neat turns of the brown silk to form the rib. Secure the silk and cut away any surplus. On top of the hook tie in a slip of brown mottled Turkey feather for the wingcase. Dub the tying thread with some more beaver fur for the thorax.

3

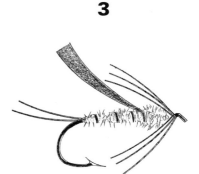

Wind on the thorax and tie on a Partridge hackle.

4

Bring the Turkey feather over the thorax. This divides and separates the Partridge hackle fibres so that they extend on either side of the hook. Finish the fly in the usual way.

Red Ibis

This fly can best be described as a Cardinal without the wing. It is an attractor nymph based on the colour red, which attracts all species of trout. It works especially well if the fish are feeding on bloodworms.

Hook: *Down-eyed 10-14*
Thread: *Pre-waxed red*
Tail: *Bright-red cock-hackle fibres*
Body: *Bright-red seal's fur or substitute*
Rib: *Fine oval silver tinsel or wire*
Hackle: *Soft bright-red hen*
Head: *Red*

1

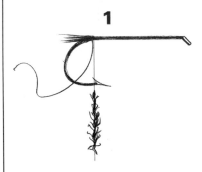

Take the thread down the shank to the bend and tie in a bunch of bright-red cock-hackle fibres. At the same place tie in a length of the fine oval silver tinsel for the rib. Dub some red seal's fur or substitute onto the thread.

2

Take the fur-laden thread back up the shank and form a carrot-shaped body. Follow this with the rib, tie off, and remove any surplus.

3

Wind on the soft bright-red hen hackle. Finish the fly in the usual way.

Red Spot Shrimp

This pattern was created by Neil Patterson to imitate the *Gammarus* species of freshwater shrimp, complete with an egg cluster within its body. This pattern is effective on rivers and on still water. The fluorescent spots make the fly highly visible in murky conditions.

The original dressing called for a gold-wire rib under the back. Sometimes it is more effective to use a clear monofilament nylon and rib it over the back. This gives a more realistic fly, with the rib emphasizing the natural segmentation of a crustacean's back.

Hook: *Down-eyed or shrimp hook 8-14*
Thread: *Pre-waxed olive*
Body: *Olive seal's fur or substitute*
Spot: *Red fluorescent wool or floss yarn*
Rib: *Gold wire or clear nylon*
Back: *Clear plastic sheet (polythene)*
Head: *Olive*

1

Take the thread half-way down the shank and tie in a length of the red fluorescent wool or floss yarn at right-angles across the back.

2

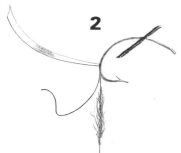

Continue the thread down the shank to the bend and there tie in the ribbing medium. Also tie in a strip of the clear polythene for the back. Dub the olive fur onto the thread.

3

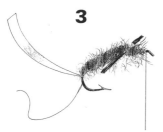

Take the fur-laden thread down the shank to form the body, making sure that the red wool is not trapped, but still projects on either side.

4

Take the rib (if you use gold wire) up the shank. Follow this with the clear polythene for the back. Alternatively, tie the polythene over the back, secure it at the head, and then rib it with the clear nylon rib.

Finally trim the red wool flush with the sides to achieve the spotting effect. Whip finish the head and varnish.

Reed Smut Nymph

The Reed Smut or *Similium* midges of various species are often taken by trout. This pattern, to imitate the nymph of these small flies, was created by the famous Danish flytier, Preben Torp Jacobsen, whose work is internationally acknowledged.

Hook: *Down-eyed 16-18*
Thread: *Pre-waxed brown*
Underbody: *Copper wire*
Body: *In three parts: the first is tapered at one end and is of oval silver tinsel; the middle part is of blood-red seal's fur (or substitute); and the third is tapered at the other end and also of oval silver tinsel.*
Head: *Brown*

1

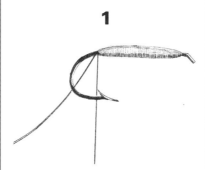

Using copper wire form an underbody tapered at both ends. Then take the thread down to the bend of the hook and tie in a length of oval silver tinsel.

2

Take the thread one third of the way up the shank and follow this with the oval silver tinsel. Dub the blood-red seal's fur or substitute onto the thread.

3

Tie in another length of oval silver tinsel, take the fur-laden thread to the eye of the hook and follow with the tinsel, forming a reverse taper. Complete the fly with the usual whip finish and varnish.

Sepia Nymph

This fly imitates the larval stage of the mayfly *Leptophlebia marginata* and was named by C. F. Walker the Sepia Dun. He described it in his book *Lake Flies and Their Imitation*. This fly is a common species found on many still waters in Great Britain. It is an active swimming nymph and the adult usually hatches towards the end of May.

Hook: *Down-eyed 10-14*
Thread: *Pre-waxed brown*
Tail: *Black hen or cock hackle fibres as long as the body and tied so that they splay out slightly*
Body: *Dark-brown seal's fur (or substitute) with the addition of a little ginger fur*
Rib: *Fine silver tinsel*
Thorax: *Black seal's fur or substitute*
Hackle: *Dark brown hen*
Head: *Brown*

Follow the instructions as for the Quill Gordon Nymph (page 31) and substitute the appropriate materials.

Sharpe's Favourite

This pattern is a modern sedge pupa pattern devised by Jim Sharpe and popularized by Bob Carnill in his regular column in the magazine "Trout Fisherman". The fly itself is a little too highly coloured to be a natural imitation of a specific sedge pupa. Nevertheless the fly is a proven fish-taker during a sedge rise.

Hook: *Caddis hook*
Thread: *Pre-waxed olive*
Body: *Brick-red seal's fur or substitute*
Rib: *Gold wire*
Thorax: *Medium-green seal's fur or substitute*
Wingcase: *Grey Mallard quill*
Hackle: *Hot-orange cock hackle*
Head: *Olive*

1

Take the tying thread down the shank and around the bend of the hook. There tie in a length of the gold wire. Dub the brick-red seal's fur onto the thread.

2

Take the fur-laden thread back along the shank to the point shown and follow this with the gold wire. There tie in the grey Mallard quill for the wingcase. Now dub the medium-green seal's fur onto the tying thread.

3

Form the thorax by winding on the fur-laden thread. Take the grey Mallard quill over the back of the thorax and secure. Cut away any surplus.

4

Tie in a few fibres of hot-orange cock hackle beneath the hook, finish with a neat, small head, and varnish.

Suspender Buzzer

This pattern was created by John Goddard after the Natant Nymph pattern described by Charles E. Brooks in his book *Nymph Fishing for Larger Trout*. This pattern can be tied in a wide range of colours. We show the orange dressing here.

Hook: *Down-eyed 10-14*
Thread: *Orange*
Tail: *White fluorescent wool*
Body: *Orange seal's fur or substitute*
Rib: *Flat silver tinsel*
Thorax: *Brown Turkey herl*
Suspender: *A ball of plastazote or a polystyrene bead, held in a piece of nylon stocking*
Head: *Orange*

1

Cut a small portion of nylon stocking to hold the plastic bead. I have found beads the most convenient, as they come pre-rounded and require no shaping.

2

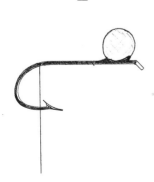

Take the thread down the hook a little way and tie in the nylon piece containing the bead. Continue the thread down the hook.

3

At the bend of the hook tie in a tuft of white fluorescent wool and the flat silver tinsel. Dub the orange fur onto the thread.

4

Form the body by taking the fur-laden thread up the shank and follow it with the tinsel. Tie in a strip of brown Turkey herl.

5

Form the thorax, cut off any surplus Turkey herl and form a neat head. Finish in the usual way.

Swannundaze Stonefly Larva

The hatches of large stoneflies on the freestone rivers of the American West provide the flyfisherman with some of the finest sport to be found anywhere in the world. Many anglers move from river to river following such hatches. Stoneflies *(Plecoptera)* favour cold, rock-and-boulder strewn streams and rivers, free of pollution (for which they have very little tolerance). This particular nymphal pattern can be used to represent the larva of such species as the *Pteronarcys* or the Big Golden Stonefly *(Petronarcella)*.

Though this realistic fly may seem a little complex to tie, by following the various stages it should pose no great difficulty.

Hook: *Down-eyed 4-12 long shank*
Thread: *Pre-waxed brown*
Tail: *Brown Goose biots (see note) or Ringneck Pheasant tail fibres*
Body: *Dark transparent amber Swannundaze (see note)*
Rib: *Brown Ostrich herl*
Thorax: *Amber translucent dubbing or polypropylene*
Legs: *Brown speckled hen fibres*
Wingcases: *Speckled hen-body feathers*
Head: *Brown*

Goose biots

These feathers are the small stiff fibres found on the leading edge of a Goose's primary wing feather. They make ideal tails and also legs for some nymphs.

Swannundaze

This is the trade name given to a plastic strip which is flat on one side and curved on the other. It was introduced to the fly-fishing world by Frank Johnson of New Jersey. It comes in a wide range of transparent and opaque colours and makes a very natural-looking body for a wide range of aquatic nymphs. It is available in three widths, and it is the medium width that is generally used. I understand that its name was taken from the combined names of Frank Johnson's children.

1

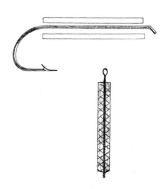

First it is necessary to weight the fly. Place two pieces of lead wire on either side of the hook and tie on. Flatten into shape with a pair of pliers.

2

Take the thread down the hook to the bend. Dub on a small pinch of the amber dubbing to separate the two tail biots, which you tie in on either side of the hook.

3

Prepare the Swannundaze before tying it in. First cut the end of the plastic into a point. I have always found it beneficial to serrate the end to prevent pull-out. This is easily done by nibbling the end slightly with your teeth.

4

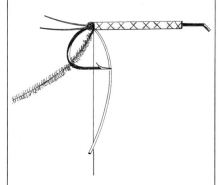

Tie in the Swannundaze and a length of the brown Ostrich herl for the rib.

5

Wind on the Swannundaze to the point shown and follow this with the Ostrich herl, which should fall between the turns of Swannundaze. Dub some more of the amber thorax fur onto the tying thread.

6

Prepare the hen-body feathers for the wingcases. I do this by pulling the feathers into a slim shape after soaking them in varnish. When they are dry, cut the ends into a V.

7

Take a turn of the dubbed thread around the shank. Tie in a few fibres of brown, speckled hen fibres on either side of the hook to simulate the legs. Take another turn of the dubbed thread around the shank and tie in the first of the wingcases.

8

Repeat the leg procedure twice, each followed by another turn of dubbed thread. Take the wingcase over the final dubbing to form the head of the fly.

Basically, the thorax portion has three sets of legs, three turns of dubbing, and two flat wingcases. Finally, a portion of the second wingcase feather is tied down.

9

Remove any surplus feather fibre, whip finish, and varnish. The drawing shows the finished fly from above.

Walker's Mayfly Nymph

This nymph, created by the late Richard Walker, is one of the most popular nymphs in use today, even on waters that do not have a mayfly hatch. It is usually fished heavily weighted. The original pattern used Ostrich herl, but most patterns nowadays use angora or other similar wools.

Hook: *Down-eyed 8-12 long shank*
Thread: *Pre-waxed brown*
Tail: *Cock Pheasant tail fibres*
Body: *Creamy yellow angora wool or similar*
Rib: *Brown yarn*
Thorax: *As body*
Wingcase: *Cock Pheasant tail fibres*
Legs: *The tips of the cock Pheasant tail fibres used for the wingcase, divided on either side of the body*

1

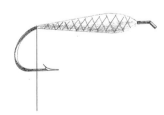

It is usual to fish this as a weighted pattern, so wind on some lead wire, or form the weighting from strips of lead foil. If lead wire is used, flatten it afterwards with a pair of pliers.

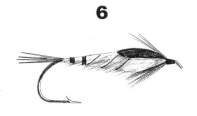

3

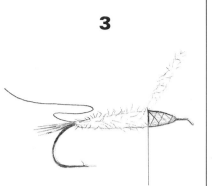

Take the tying thread back along the shank about two thirds of the way. Wrap the wool around the shank to form the body, secure, but do not cut off the excess. You need this for the thorax.

4

The rib differs from many other ribs inasmuch as it tries to emulate the two bands found on the real insect. Take the ribbing yarn and tie four very close turns. Leave a small gap and repeat. Complete the ribbing in the usual way. Earlier variations used cock Pheasant tail fibre for the banding, but the brown yarn is much easier.

6

Take the thread towards the eye, and wind on the balance of the wool to complete the thorax, tie off, and cut away the surplus. Take the cock Pheasant tail fibres over the thorax and tie off. Divide the fibres on either side of the hook and secure. Complete the fly in the usual way.

7

The fly viewed from above. To finish the fly, coat the back and underneath the hook with PVC varnish. When dry, the top and underside of the fly are smooth but the hair from the wool can be picked out at the sides to resemble breathing filaments.

2

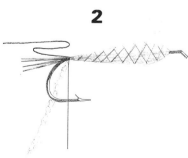

Take the tying thread down the shank and there tie in the cock Pheasant tail fibres, a length of brown yarn, and the wool for the body.

5

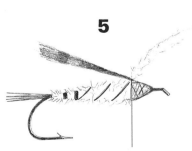

After ribbing the body as shown, tie on top of the hook a generous bunch of cock Pheasant tail fibres for the wingcase and for the subsequent legs. Tie these fibres in by the root and not the tip.

Water Tiger

Both the larva and the adult of the large water beetle *Dytiscus marginalis* are voracious predators. They will seize all manner of insects as well as small fish. In weedy areas this beetle and its larvae are often preyed on by trout. The aptly named Water Tiger is a fair representation of the *Dytiscus* larva. The fully developed natural nymph can be almost 75 mm (3") long.

Hook: *Down-eyed 8-10 long shank*
Thread: *Brown*
Tail: *Tip of body material*
Body: *Pale sepia Condor herl (a cinnamon Turkey herl will substitute)*
Rib and Gills: *Peacock herl and copper wire*
Thorax: *Light brown fur*
Hackle: *Brown Partridge*
Wingcase: *Same as body*
Head: *Brown*

1

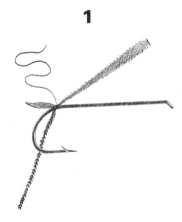

Take the thread down the shank to the bend and tie in the Condor substitute so that it projects beyond the hook as a tail. At the same point tie in a length of copper wire and a strip of Peacock herl.

2

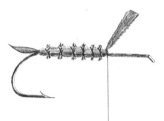

Take the thread two-thirds of the way back up the shank. Follow with the herl for the body and then with even, spaced turns of Peacock herl and finally, the copper wire, keeping the wire close to the Peacock herl. Do not cut off the excess body herl; this will form the wingcase. Cut off excess Peacock herl and copper wire.

3

Dub some light brown fur onto the tying thread and wind it around the hook to form a thorax. Tie in a brown Partridge hackle and wind it on.

4

Take the wingcase material over the back of the thorax and tie off. This divides the Partridge hackle naturally, so that the hackle fibres project on either side of the thorax. Trim off any excess herl, form a neat head, and finish the fly in the usual way.

II
DRY FLIES

August Dun

This fly is sometimes called the Autumn Dun and it is tied to represent a largish mayfly (*Ecdyonorus dispar*) which occurs mostly in the western areas of Britain. Closely allied species are found in many waters in Europe. At first glance, they are similar in appearance to the March Brown. The dressing given here was created by Roger Wooley.

Hook: *Up-eyed 10-14*
Thread: *Pre-waxed sherry spinner*
Tail: *Dark-ginger cock-hackle fibres*
Body: *Medium-brown floss silk*
Rib: *Yellow silk*
Wing: *Hen Pheasant wing quill*
Hackle: *Dark-ginger cock*
Head: *Brown*

1

Take the thread down the shank to the bend and tie in the dark-ginger cock-hackle fibres for the tail. At the same place tie in a length of yellow silk for the rib. Return the thread up the shank to the position shown in the sketch and there tie in two slips of hen Pheasant wing quill taken from left and right feathers. Tie the wing upright. The natural twist to the feather usually separates the two slips. Tie in a length of medium-brown floss silk behind the wing.

2

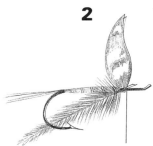

Form the body by taking the medium-brown floss silk down to the bend and back. Follow with the yellow silk for the rib. Tie off and cut off the surplus. Tie in a dark-ginger cock hackle by the stalk.

3

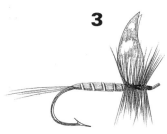

Wind on the hackle, taking a few turns behind the wing and the rest in front. Secure the hackle and remove any surplus feather. Finish the fly in the usual way.

Black Gnat

One of the most popular dry flies in use by both river and still-water fishermen. There are many dressings that try to imitate this particular insect of the *Bibio* species. It is closely allied to the Hawthorn Fly and also to the Heather Fly.

Hook: *Up-eyed 12-16*
Thread: *Pre-waxed black*
Tail: *Black cock-hackle fibres*
Body: *Stripped Peacock quill*
Thorax: *Black fur*
Hackle: *Black cock*
Wing: *Starling*
Head: *Black*

1

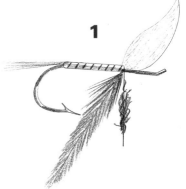

Having already tied in the wing, tail, and body in the usual way, tie in a black cock hackle by the tip. Dub some black fur onto the tying thread.

2

Wind the fur-laden thread down the shank towards the eye, behind and in front of the wings.

3

Wind on the hackle and complete the fly in the usual way.

Black Palmer

There are a number of different dressings for the fly called the Black Palmer, and this particular pattern uses a dark-furnace hackle. Others use an all-black hackle. Palmer-dressed flies are among some of the oldest artificial flies still in use today. This is an excellent pattern when fished as a bob fly in a team of three when fishing lakes and reservoirs.

Hook: *Down-eyed 8-12*
Thread: *Pre-waxed black*
Body: *Black Ostrich herl*
Rib: *Gold tinsel*
Hackle: *Dark furnace*
Head: *Black*

Follow the instructions for the other palmer-dressed flies (see, for instance, the Bibio, page 74) and substitute the materials given above.

Blue Bottle

Sometimes, flies such as blue bottles, cow dung flies, and other terrestrial flies are blown onto the water. When this happens trout will take them as opportunity food. This traditional Irish pattern represents one of these rather unsavoury creatures.

Hook: *Up-eyed 10-12*
Thread: *Pre-waxed black*
Body: *Blue floss silk*
Rib: *Iron-blue dun or black hackle*
Wings: *Cree hackle tips*
Hackle: *Iron-blue dun or black*
Head: *Black*

1

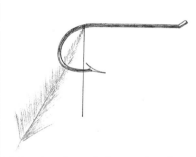

Take the thread down the shank to the bend and tie in the ribbing hackle.

2

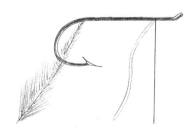

Return the thread back along the shank and tie in a length of blue floss silk.

3

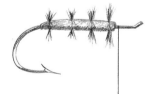

Form the body by winding the floss silk down the shank and back again. Rib this floss with the hackle, palmer-fashion. Tie off and cut away any surplus hackle. Trim the hackle all around.

4

Select two Cree hackle tips and tie them flat on top of the hook in "delta fashion".

5

Wind on the front iron blue-dun or black hackle. Complete the fly in the usual manner.

Blue Dun

There are many patterns named Blue Dun. They are used dry throughout the flyfishing world as an imitation of the Olives. However, they can also be used to imitate smaller sizes of various midges.

Hook: *Up-eyed 12-18*
Thread: *Pre-waxed black or yellow*
Tail: *Blue-dun cock-hackle fibres*
Body: *Mole or rabbit under-body fur*
Rib: *Silver wire*
Wing: *Starling*
Hackle: *Blue dun*
Head: *Black*

Follow the instructions for any of the winged dry flies, such as Pink Lady (page 64), and substitute the appropriate materials.

Blue Upright

A West Country pattern from Devon, created by R. S. Austin, this is used to imitate a number of light-coloured Olives. This is another of those patterns which are first fished dry and then wet after they have become water-logged.

Hook: *Up-eyed 12-16*
Thread: *Pre-waxed black or purple*
Tail: *Medium-blue dun cock hackle fibres*
Body: *Well-marked stripped Peacock quill*
Hackle: *Medium blue dun cock*
Head: *Black*

Sometimes this pattern is dressed using a honey cock hackle and tail.

1

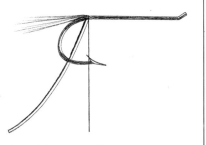

Take the thread down the hook to the bend and there tie in a bunch of medium-blue dun hackle fibres for the tail. At the same point tie in a well-marked stripped Peacock quill (see note on stripping quills, page 21).

2

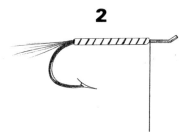

Return the thread back up the shank and follow it with the Peacock quill to form a neat body.

3

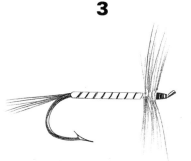

Wind on a medium-blue dun hackle (two hackles for the larger hook sizes) and complete the fly in the usual way.

Caenis Spinner

This pattern was devised by the innovative British flytier Stewart Canham, who worked closely with John Goddard and Brian Clarke on their excellent book *The Trout and the Fly*, which was also an absorbing television programme. This fly is a more realistic imitation of the natural insect than the Last Hope (page 58).

Hook: *Up-eyed 18-20*
Thread: *Pre-waxed white*
Tail: *White cock-hackle fibres*
Body: *White polythene*
Thorax: *Brown Turkey herl (a substitute for Condor)*
Hackle: *White cock hackle*
Wing: *White hen hackle*
Head: *White*

1

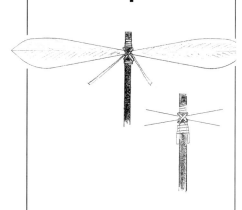

Take two white hen hackles and cut them to shape with wing cutters or shape them with wing burners. Then take the thread along the shank and tie these feathers in at the point shown. Separate them by means of a figure-of-eight knot (see detail).

2

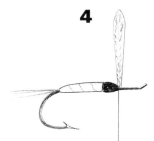

Take the thread down the shank to the bend and there tie in three white cock-hackle fibres for the tail and a strip of the white polythene. Return the thread back up the shank.

3

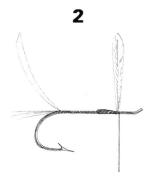

Wind the polythene up the shank to form the body, tie off and cut away any surplus. Tie in a strand of Turkey herl for the thorax.

4

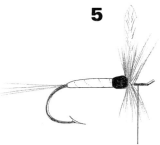

Wind on the thorax and tie off.

5

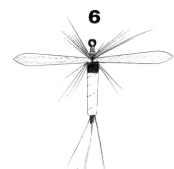

Wind on the white cock hackle with a couple of turns behind the wing and the rest in front.

6

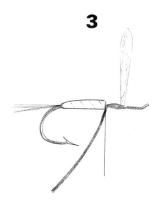

Finish the fly in the usual way. The drawing shows the fly from the top. Note the configuration of the tail and the wing.

Caperer (Welshman's Button)

There has always been a slight confusion regarding this pattern created by W. J. Lunn, the famous keeper of the River Test. The sedge called the Caperer is a largish insect of an overall light brown, while the so-called Welshman's Button is a much smaller and darker sedge. Why he should have combined both names in one artificial is a mystery and why he should place a ring of yellow colour in the middle of his fly compounds the mystery, as neither of these natural sedges have a yellow ring.

Hook: *Up-eyed size 12-14*
Thread: *Pre-waxed crimson*
Body: *Dark-cinnamon Turkey tail with a centre ring of yellow Goose fibre*
Hackles: *Black cock followed by Rhode Island Red*
Wing: *Coot quill dyed chocolate brown*
Head: *Crimson*

This fly can be tied with split wings to simulate a fluttering caddis or with wings swept back in the more usual sedge-fly configuration. Follow the instructions for the Pink Lady (page 64) and substitute with the appropriate materials.

Dogsbody

Harry Powell was a hairdresser as well as an excellent flytier. this pattern was first created in 1924, and the original fly used hair from a dog belonging to one of Mr Powell's customers. The Dogsbody was originally used on Harry Powell's local river, the Usk.

Hook: *Up-eyed 12-16*
Thread: *Pre-waxed brown*
Tail: *Three cock Pheasant tail fibres*
Body: *Camel-coloured dog's body hair or substitute*
Rib: *Fine oval gold tinsel*
Hackle: *Natural-red cock hackle and a grizzle hackle wound together or as two separate hackles (grizzle followed by the red). A well-marked Cree hackle can also be used to the same effect.*
Head: *Brown*

1

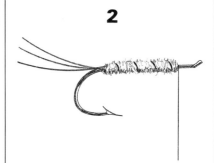

Take the thread down the hook to the bend and tie in three cock Pheasant tail fibres for the tail. At the same place tie in a length of fine oval gold tinsel for the rib and then dub the thread with the camel-coloured hair.

2

Take the fur-laden thread back up the shank and then rib carefully with the fine oval gold tinsel.

3

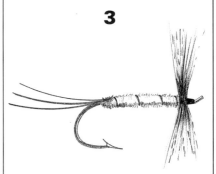

Wind on the hackles and complete the fly.

Dun Variant

Quill-bodied flies are favoured by many fly dressers, mainly due to their lightness and appearance (they resemble the natural segmentation of an insect's body). There was no greater advocate of quill-bodied dry flies than the originator of this particular pattern, the famous American fly dresser, Art Flick.

Hook: *Down-eyed 12-16*
Thread: *Pre-waxed olive*
Tail: *Dark dun hackle fibres*
Body: *A stripped hackle stalk from a red cock*
Hackle: *Dark dun cock (usually tied quite long)*
Head: *Olive*

Follow the instructions for the Blue Upright (page 44) and substitute the appropriate materials

Eric's Beetle

This fly was created by Eric Horsfall-Turner to represent a small terrestrial beetle. The fly can be fished wet or dry and is equally good for trout or grayling. Other patterns of similar appearance representing beetles are Coch-y-Bondhu, Little Chap, Fern Web, and Marlow Buzz. Eric's Beetle differs from all these by having an orange "attractor" tail. The fly resembles another favourite North Country pattern, the Treacle Parkin.

Hook: *Down-eyed for wet, up-eyed for dry 8-14*
Thread: *Black*
Tail: *Fluorescent orange wool*
Body: *Bronze Peacock herl*
Hackle: *Black hen for wet, cock for dry*

1

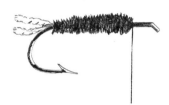

After taking the thread down the shank, tie in a tuft of the fluorescent orange wool for the tail. At the same point tie in three or four bronze Peacock herls.

2

Twist the herl and the thread to form a rope and wind this up the shank to form the body. Tie off and cut away any surplus herl.

3

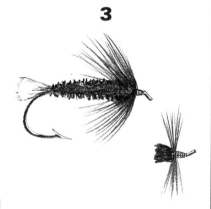

Wind on a black hackle in the usual way. On the wet fly the hackle is hen and slopes back, on the dry it is cock and upright. The dry hackle is shown on the up-eyed hook.

Europea 12

This is just one of a series of flies under the appellation Europea. Most are fine broad-spectrum imitations of sedge, or caddis, flies. The patterns are popular right through Europe and are very reminiscent of Irish or Welsh flies in their style and in the materials used in their make-up. They are usually fished dry, whereas their Celtic counterparts are generally fished wet.

Hook: *Up- or down-eyed 10-14*
Thread: *Pre-waxed yellow*
Tail: *Brown cock-hackle fibres*
Body: *Grey/brown rabbit fur*
Rib: *Yellow thread*
Wing: *Bronze Mallard*
Hackle: *Brown cock hackle*
Head: *Yellow*

1

Take the tying thread down the shank to the bend and there tie in the cock-hackle fibres for the tail. At the same point tie in a length of yellow thread for the rib. Dub the rabbit fur onto the tying thread.

2

Take the fur-laden thread back up the shank and follow this with the ribbing thread. Secure the rib and cut off any surplus.

3

Tie in the bronze Mallard wing.

4

Wind on the hackle and complete the fly in the usual way.

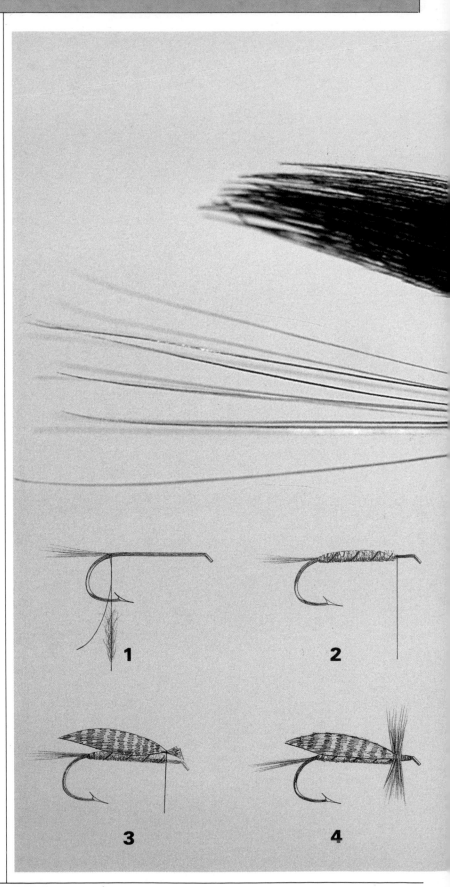

Floating Snail

Still-water pulmonate snails have the ability to absorb oxygen through their skins while in the water. They also can take in free air beneath their mantles. Quite often they are to be found in the surface film taking in air. It is then that the trout feed selectively on them. This floating pattern was devised by Cliff Henry, who collaborated with John Goddard on many still-water fly patterns.

Hook: *Down-eyed 10-14 (wide gape)*
Thread: *Black*
Body: *Shaped cork, balsa, or plastazote, covered with stripped Peacock herl; two turns of unstripped Peacock herl at the head end*

1

Cut the body material to the shape shown and slit it through three-quarters of the way.

2

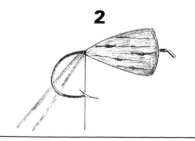

Glue the balsa securely to the hook and tie in a couple of stripped Peacock herls at the tail end.

3

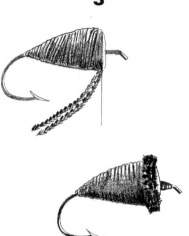

Wrap the body with the stripped herl and tie in a couple of normal Peacock herls at the head. Tie off, whip finish, and varnish.

The stripped herl can be varnished to prolong the life of the fly.

Furnace

The pattern for this very simple hackled dry fly was given by Halford in his book *Floating Flies and How to Dress Them* (1886). He thought it an excellent pattern for hot weather conditions. It was especially recommended for grayling.

Hook: *Up-eyed 14-16*
Thread: *Light brown*
Body: *Orange floss silk*
Rib: *Peacock sword herl*
Hackle: *Furnace cock (red with black list)*
Head: *Light brown*

FURNACE

1

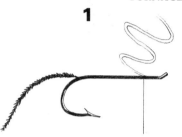

Take the thread down the shank to the bend and tie in a strand of Peacock sword herl. Return the thread up the shank and tie in a length of the orange floss silk.

2

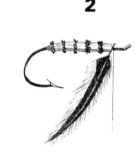

Form the body by winding the floss silk down the shank and back again. Follow this by ribbing the body with the Peacock sword herl. Tie in the furnace cock hackle.

3

Wind on the hackle. Form a neat head and complete the fly in the usual way.

Greenwell's Glory

Perhaps this fly could be considered the best-known of all dry flies. The fly is named after its creator, Canon William Greenwell of Durham, and was first tied by James Wright, the famous flytier of Tweedside. The pattern dates from 1854. The fly is used as an imitation of a number of olive-coloured mayflies, and it can be used wet or dry. An example of the nymph version is given on page 20.

Hook: *Up-eyed 12-16*
Thread: *Primrose (this is well waxed to give a dirty olive appearance)*
Body: *Formed from the tying thread*
Rib: *Fine gold wire*
Hackle: *Light furnace*
Wing: *Starling dyed to imitate Blackbird wing*
Head: *Primrose*

1

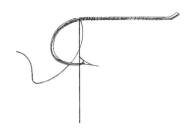

Take the well-waxed thread down the shank to the bend and there tie in a length of fine gold wire for the rib.

2

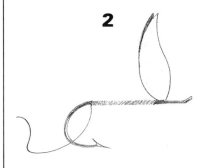

Return the thread back to the point indicated in the drawing, thus forming the body of the fly. Now, using the pinch-and-loop method, tie in a matching pair of dyed Starling wing slips and tie upright by winding behind and in front of the wings. There is no need to take turns of thread between the wing slips because the natural curvature of the feather usually separates the two wings. A needle slipped between the wings after the fly is completed, ensures separation.

3

Wind on the fine gold wire.

4

Wind on the hackle, taking two turns behind the wing and the rest in front. Finish off the fly in the usual way.

Some patterns for Greenwell's Glory call for a tail. Although not correct, this can be a useful feature, helping to balance the pattern and aiding its floating potential. All natural mayflies possess such appendages.

Hackle-point Coachman

A popular pattern on both sides of the Atlantic, this is a dry version of the famous Coachman fly, which uses lighter, see-through hackle points for the wings instead of the more conventional white duck-quill segments.

Hook: *Up-eyed 10-14*
Thread: *Brown*
Body: *Bronze Peacock herl*
Wings: *Two white cock-hackle tips*
Hackle: *Natural-red cock hackle*
Head: *Brown*

1

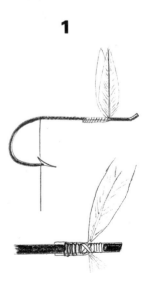

Select two white matching cock-hackle tips. Place them convex-side to convex-side and tie them in on top of the hook with a fig-ure-of-eight whip (see the en-largement).

2

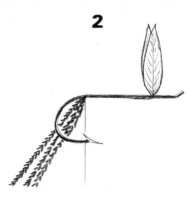

Take the thread down the shank to the bend and tie in three strands of bronze Peacock herl.

3

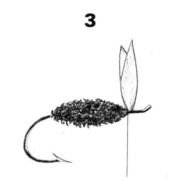

Form a rope of the thread and the Peacock herl and wind it up the shank, leaving a small gap before you get to the wings. It is at this point you tie in the hackle by its stalk.

4

Wind on the hackle and trim off any excess feather. Form a neat head and finish the fly in the normal manner.

Hackle-point Mayfly

This simple mayfly pattern can imitate both the dun and the spinner stages in the life cycle of the most famous of the angler's insects. The fly was devised by Dave Collyer, the well-known British flytier. I have used this pattern and found it as good as any of the established mayfly imitations.

Hook: *Up-eyed 10*
Thread: *Pre-waxed olive*
Tail: *Cock Pheasant tail fibres*
Body: *Natural raffia*
Rib: *Oval gold tinsel*
Wing: *Two large and two small badger cock hackles (if you want, you may use only the larger hackles and dispense with the two rear small hackles)*
Hackle: *Iron-blue dun cock hackle*
Head: *Olive*

1

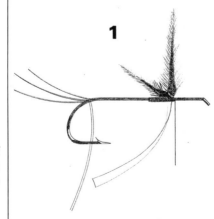

Select two small and two larger badger cock hackles for the wings. Take the thread down the shank to the bend and tie in three cock Pheasant tail fibres for the tail. At the same point tie in a length of oval gold tinsel for the rib. Return the thread up the shank and there tie in the two sets of badger cock-hackle wings, the smaller wings to the rear. When secured and the stalks tied in (see Caenis Spinner, page 45), tie in a length of natural raffia.

2

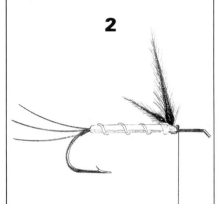

Form the body by winding the raffia down the hook shank and back. Follow this with even turns of the oval gold tinsel, tie off, and cut away any surplus tinsel and raffia.

3

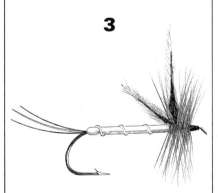

Tie in a iron-blue dun cock hackle and wind on a couple of turns behind the wings. Continue winding the hackle in front of the wings, tie off, cut away any surplus feather, and complete the fly in the usual way.

Half Stone

A classic fly from the west of England, given by R. S. Austin for fishing the streams and rivers of Devon. It was also mentioned by Halford in his *Floating Flies and How to Tie Them*. It is fished as both a wet fly and a dry fly. In fact it is a common practice to start fishing the fly as a dry pattern, and, once it is swamped, to continue to fish it as a wet fly.

Hook: *Up-eyed 12-14*
Thread: *Black*
Tail: *Sparse blue-dun cock-hackle fibres*
Body: *Rear two-thirds yellow floss silk, final third grey mole fur*
Hackle: *Blue dun, either palmered through the mole fur or tied as a conventional hackle*
Head: *Black*

1

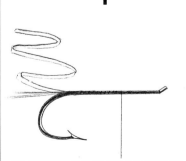

Take the thread down the shank to the bend of the hook and tie in the blue-dun cock-hackle fibres for the tail. At the same spot tie in the length of yellow floss and return the thread two-thirds of the way up the shank.

2

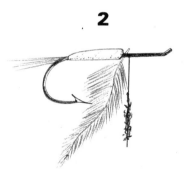

Wind on the yellow floss silk, tie off and cut away any surplus. Dub a pinch of grey mole fur onto the tying thread.

3

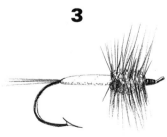

Palmer the hackle through the mole fur or tie it in as usual. Form a neat head, whip finish, and varnish.

Hawthorn

The natural Hawthorn fly *(Bibio marci)* appears in its native Great Britain in the month of May and can be an important fly for both the river and still-water angler, for it can occur in very large numbers. It is a close relative of the Black Gnat *(Bibio johannis)*. Another closely allied *Bibio* species is *Bibio pomonae*, the Heather Fly or Bloody Doctor, which emerges from June onwards in some areas. I shall give the dressing for this pattern also, as it is virtually the same as the Hawthorn. See also York's Favourite (page 70), which is a Welsh pattern used on the Welsh lakes during the Heather Fly time.

Hook: *Up-eyed 12*
Thread: *Pre-waxed black*
Body: *Peacock herl*
Trailing Legs: *Swan or Goose dyed black*
Wing: *Two pale-blue hackle points*
Hackle: *Black cock*
Head: *Black*

To imitate the Heather Fly, substitute the black Swan legs with cock Pheasant tail strands and the black hackle with a dark-furnace cock hackle.

1

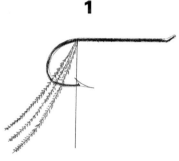

Take the thread down the shank to the bend and tie in three strands of the Peacock herl.

2

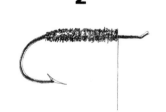

Form a rope of the herl and the tying thread and wind it up the shank to form the body. Secure and cut off any surplus herl.

3

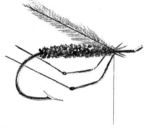

Take two strands of the dyed black Swan or Goose fibre and tie a knot in each. Attach these simulated legs to either side of the body. On top of the hook tie in two pale-blue hackle points for the wings. These can be tied so that they splay outwards, or they can be tied flat on top of the hook.

4

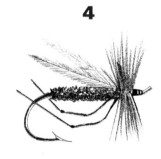

Wind on a black cock hackle, whip finish, and varnish.

Heather Moth

The Heather Moth is just one of a number of flies tied to represent members of the *Lepidoptera* family. The Ermine, the White Moth, and the Hoolet are just three other such moth patterns. All of them are excellent flies to use at dusk for both trout and sea trout. This pattern is adorned with a tail, which is added for balance. The real insect, of course, has no tail. The fly does not imitate a specific insect but can be used to imitate any light-coloured moth found on the water. This pattern is credited to an Edward Davies, about 1950.

Hook: *Up-eyed 8-12*
Thread: *Black*
Tail: *Barred Teal feather fibres*
Body: *Grey/blue-dun seal's fur or substitute*
Rib: *Oval silver tinsel*
Hackle: *Grizzle (Plymouth Rock); sometimes, badger is used*
Head: *Black*

Though this is a dry fly, it is tied in the same way as the palmered wet flies given, for instance, Golden Olive Bumble (page 86). The hackle for the dry fly is tied more upright than that for the wet patterns.

Herefordshire Alder

This is a Welsh-border pattern, intended to imitate the natural Alder fly *(Sialis lutaria)*. Unlike many other imitations of this insect, this fly is a hackled pattern. As you can see from the photograph, it is sometimes given a tail for balance. The natural insect has no tail.

This pattern was introduced to me by Ralph Perry many years ago when we used to fish the various Welsh border rivers. He was huntsman for the Croome Hunt for many years, and his great love was fly fishing. Although the pattern was in evidence for many years before our success with it, it has become, along with the Leckford Professor (page 58), the most successful dry fly that I have used on any river.

Hook: *Up-eyed 12-14*
Thread: *Pre-waxed yellow or black*
Tail *(optional)*: *Medium blue-dun hackle fibres.*
Body: *Cock Pheasant centre tail*
Hackle: *Medium-blue dun cock hackle*
Head: *Yellow*

This is a very simple fly to tie. Simply follow the instructions for the Pheasant Tail (page 63) and substitute the appropriate materials.

Hornberg

This is a versatile fly. It can be used as a sub-surface lure (when it presumably imitates a small bait fish), or it can be used dry as a sedge pattern. I have used it successfully in both ways. It was devised in Portage County, Wisconsin, by Frank Hornberg, and it is used right up into Canada. It is normally tied on long-shank hooks but, in recent years, mini-versions tied on small, conventional hooks have become popular with some anglers.

Hook: *Down-eyed 8-12 long shank*
Thread: *Pre-waxed black*
Body: *Flat silver Lurex or Mylar tinsel*
Wing: *Two silver Mallard flank feathers flanking two yellow cock hackles (some modern versions use an inner wing of yellow hair)*
Cheek *(optional)*: *Jungle Cock*
Hackle: *Grizzle*
Head: *Black*

1

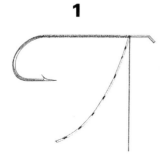

Take the thread down the shank to the bend and back. Tie in a length of the body tinsel chosen.

2

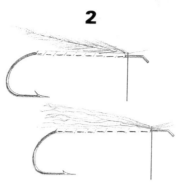

Wrap the tinsel around the shank down to the bend and back again, forming the body. Secure the tinsel and remove any surplus. On top of the hook tie in two yellow cock hackles, back-to-back, or, if so desired, a bunch of yellow hair.

3

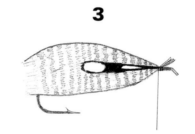

Pre-prepare two silver Mallard feathers in the same way as in the Gray Ghost (page 113), by carefully sticking the Jungle Cock cheek to the sides. Attach these feathers on either side of the hook, flanking the inner yellow wing.

4

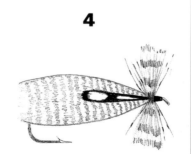

Finally wind on a grizzle hackle as a collar. Complete the fly with the usual finish and a dab of varnish.

Houghton Ruby

This fly was devised by William J. Lunn, keeper on the Houghton stretch of the River Test. It is used as a representation of the female Iron Blue Spinner (imago). It is excellent for grayling.

Hook: *Up-eyed 12-16*
Thread: *Crimson*
Tail: *White cock-hackle fibres*
Body: *A white cock-hackle stem dyed crimson or scarlet (these days it is easier to mark with a waterproof ink of the appropriate colour)*
Hackle: *Rhode Island Red cock hackle*
Wing: *Two blue-dun hen-hackle tips tied spent*
Head: *Crimson*

1

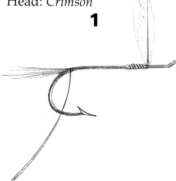

This fly is tied in much the same way as the Hackle-point Coachman (page 52) but instead of the wings being left upright, they are tied to stick out horizontally (spent). Tie in the two blue-dun hackle tips, as for the Hackle-point Coachman. Wind the thread down the hook to the bend and tie in the white cock-hackle fibres for the tail and the white cock-hackle stem.

2

Return the thread up the shank and form the body by winding the hackle stem up the hook.

3

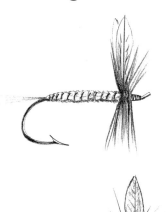

Tie in the Rhode Island Red hackle behind the wing and wind it on. Tie off and cut away any surplus feather. Force the wings down onto the horizontal plane. Finish the fly as usual.

Lake Olive Dun

This fly is a hackled imitation of the mayfly (*Cloeon simile*), a fairly common species found on many still waters. This is a simple, basic dry fly and is not difficult to tie. The Condor is a protected bird so the herl can be substituted with a dyed Goose quill or similar.

Hook: *Up-eyed 12-14*
Thread: *Brown*
Tail: *Light-dun cock-hackle fibres*
Body: *Dark-olive Condor herl or substitute*
Rib: *Silver wire*
Hackle: *Medium-blue dun cock hackles*
Head: *Brown*

1

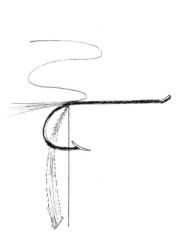

Take the thread down the shank to the bend and tie in a tail of light-dun cock-hackle fibres. Tie in a length of the silver wire, and then the Condor-herl substitute for the body.

2

Return the thread up the shank, and follow with first the herl then the silver wire.

3

Tie in two medium-blue dun cock hackles and wind on.

Note
The normal way to wind a dry-fly cock hackle is to wind it with the shiny, or convex, side facing the eye of the hook (fig A). If the hackle is wound with the dull, or concave, side facing the eye (fig B), the resultant fly will sit better on the surface, because it is better balanced.

Last Hope

This fly was created by John Goddard to imitate a number of smaller mayflies, including the Pale Watery and the curse of many fishermen, the Caenis.

Hook: *Up-eyed 16-18*
Thread: *Pre-waxed pale yellow (primrose)*
Tail: *A bunch of honey-dun cock-hackle fibres*
Body: *Two or three strands of grey Goose (as a Condor substitute)*
Hackle: *Short-fibred honey-dun cock*
Head: *Yellow*

Follow the instructions for the Pheasant Tail (page 63) and substitute the appropriate materials.

Leckford Professor

This fly was named after the Leckford stretch of the River Test in Hampshire. It was the creation of Ernest Mott, the keeper on that particular stretch. It is unusual inasmuch as the hackle is tied at the rear of the hook. Sooner or later every beginner to fly dressing ties patterns in this style, but very few of them stand the test of time. The Leckford Professor is an exception.

Hook: *Up-eyed 14-16*
Thread: *Pre-waxed sherry spinner colour (light brown)*
Body: *Hare's fur including the grey under-fur*
Rib: *Fine flat gold tinsel*
Hackle: *A natural-red and a white cock hackle*
Head: *Sherry spinner*

1

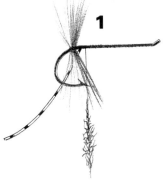

Take the thread down the shank to the bend and wind on first a white cock hackle then a red cock hackle. Tie off and cut away any surplus feather. Now tie in a length of the fine flat gold tinsel and dub some hare's fur onto the tying thread.

2

Take the fur-laden thread down the shank and follow this with the fine flat gold tinsel for the rib. Secure it and cut away any surplus. Finish the fly with the usual whip finish and varnish.

Loch Ordie

This pattern is perhaps one of the most well-known of the Scottish dapping flies. It is often tied with a flying treble to give additional hooking power. The pattern shown is without such a treble, because many people these days want the fly to float a little longer. The addition of the treble is a decided disadvantage when it comes to floating but compensates for this when it comes to hooking.

Hook: *Down-eyed 8-14*
Thread: *Pre-waxed black*
Body: *Reddish-brown cock*
Hackle: *White cock hackle*
Head: *Black*

1

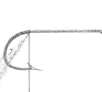

Take the thread down the shank to the bend and there tie in two reddish-brown cock hackles.

2

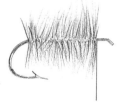

Return the thread back up the shank and then wind on the two hackles together up along the shank to form a heavily hackled body. Tie off and snip away any surplus feather fibre.

3

Tie in a white cock hackle and wind to the eye. Finish the fly with a neat head, whip finish, and varnish.

March Brown

This pattern is a popular hackled dry fly tied to represent *Rithrogena haarupi*, a species of mayfly. Most dry-fly dressings of the March Brown are winged, but this is one of the few that only uses hackles.

Hook: *Up-eyed 10-12*
Thread: *Pre-waxed brown or black*
Tail: *Ginger cock hackles*
Body: *Hare's ear*
Rib: *Yellow silk*
Hackles: *Ginger with brown Partridge in front*
Head: *Brown*

Follow the instructions for the Welsh Partridge (page 68), which is a similar fly in all respects. Simply substitute the appropriate materials.

Medium Sedge

This particular pattern was devised by Joscelyn Lane and given in his book *Lake and Loch Fishing,* published in the early 1950s. This pattern relies solely on feather fibre for the body wing and hackle.

Hook: *Down-eyed 12*
Thread: *Pre-waxed straw-coloured*
Body: *Honey cock hackle*
Wing: *Honey cock-hackle fibres over the back*
Hackle: *Honey cock hackle*
Head: *Light brown*

1

Take the thread down the hook to the bend and tie in a honey cock hackle by the tip.

2

Return the thread back up the shank and follow this with the hackle palmer-fashion. Tie off and trim away any excess material. Short-clip the hackle to shape.

3

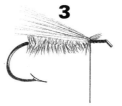

Tie in a bunch of honey cock-hackle fibres for the wing.

4

Wind on the hackle in the usual way. Whip finish and varnish. The head is tied with straw-coloured thread, which turns light brown when varnished.

Olive Dun

There are many patterns tied to represent the sub imago of a number of natural Olives, and several are called by this name. I discovered this pattern in Ireland, and the trout have found it irresistible wherever I have used it. The fly can be tied as a wet or dry pattern.

Hook: *Up-eyed 12-16*
Thread: *Pre-waxed olive*
Tail: *Olive cock-hackle fibres*
Tag: *Flat gold tinsel*
Body: *Olive seal's fur or substitute*
Rib (optional): *Fine gold wire*
Wing: *Starling*
Hackle: *Olive cock hackle*
Head: *Olive*

1

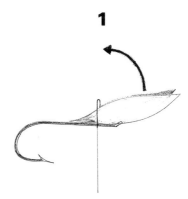

First tie in the wings, which must have a slightly forward tilt to them. To achieve this effect, the feather slips are tied so that they slope over the eye of the hook. So take the tying thread a little way down the shank to the point shown and tie in the wings by the usual pinch-and-loop method. Take the tips of the feather between thumb and finger and pull upright. Take the thread around the roots of the wing, in front and behind, so that the wings are more or less vertical but with a slight inclination toward the eye.

2

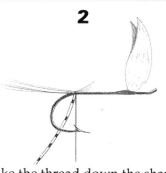

Take the thread down the shank to the bend and there tie in the olive cock-hackle fibres for the tail. At this point also tie in a length of flat gold tinsel for the tag or tip.

3

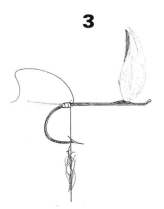

Take a few turns of the flat gold tinsel around the hook to form a small tag, secure, and cut off any surplus tinsel. Tie in a length of fine gold wire (if a rib is wanted) and dub the olive seal's fur onto the thread.

4

Take the fur-laden thread back up the shank just short of the wing. Follow this with the rib. Tie in a good olive cock hackle behind the wing.

5

Take a couple of turns of hackle behind the wing and the rest in front. Complete the fly in the usual way.

Olive Midge

This small dry fly can be used on both river and still water, because it can represent not only the smaller of the mayflies but also various other insect species, such as the Chironomid midge. The fly can also be tied in black, grey, brown, or white.

Hook: *Up-eyed 14-18*
Thread: *Pre-waxed olive*
Tail: *Light-olive cock-hackle fibres*
Body: *Grey seal's fur or substitute*
Rib: *Silver wire*
Hackle: *Light-olive cock*
Head: *Olive*

This is another pretty basic hackled dry fly. Follow instructions for the Pheasant Tail (page 63) and substitute the appropriate materials.

Olive Quill

There are a number of patterns called Olive Quill. Some are tied with a wing, others as hackled dry flies. In the fly depicted the wings have a definite backward tilt rather than being tied vertically. This is thought to give a better balance to the fly and a more realistic appearance when viewed from beneath. This pattern was created by E. J. Malone, author of *Irish Trout & Salmon Flies*, 1984.

Hook: *Up-eyed 14-16*
Thread: *Pre-waxed olive*
Tail: *Olive cock-hackle fibres*
Body: *Stripped Peacock quill*
Wing: *Starling wing quill*
Hackle: *Olive cock hackle*
Head: *Olive*

1

Take the thread down the shank to the bend and tie in a few olive cock-hackle fibres for the tail. At the same place tie in a strip of the stripped Peacock herl.

2

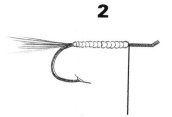

Return the thread back up the shank and follow with the stripped herl to form the body.

3

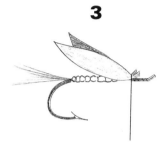

Take a slip of Starling feather from a right quill and one from a left quill and tie in on top of the hook so they slope backwards.

4

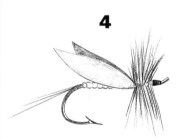

Wind on the olive cock hackle and complete the fly with the usual whip finish and varnish.

Parachute Adams

The Adams is probably one of the world's most popular dry flies. It is a broad-spectrum pattern, by which is meant that it does not imitate any specific insect but can be used to represent a wide range of aquatic flies. There are many who believe that the Adams is a good pattern to use when there is a hatch of sedge (caddis) on the water. I have used this fly as a

PARACHUTE ADAMS

good imitation of a Medium Olive. This particular version does not have the conventional hackle but utilizes the parachute form, that is to say, the hackle is wound around the root of the wing in the horizontal plane.

Hook: *Down-eyed 10-16*
Thread: *Pre-waxed grey or yellow*
Tail: *Mixed brown and grizzle hackle fibres*
Body: *Muskrat fur*
Wing: *White calf tail (the original Adams used two grizzle hackle tips as the wing)*
Hackle: *Two, one grizzle and one brown cock hackle (a well-marked Cree cock-hackle can substitute)*
Head: *Grey*

1

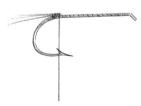

Take the thread down the hook to the bend and tie in the tail fibres.

2

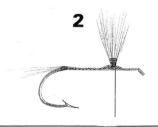

Return the thread back up the shank to the point depicted in the sketch and there tie in an upright bunch of white calf tail for the wing. Take the thread around the base of the wing. I always soak this root in quick-setting adhesive or varnish, to give a more solid base to wind on the hackle later.

3

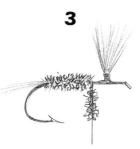

Take the thread back down the shank to the bend and dub on the muskrat fur. Take the fur-laden thread back along the shank to form the body.

4

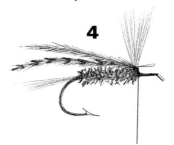

On top of the hook tie in the two cock hackles (one if you are using Cree). The hackle is tied flat on the top with the good side facing upwards.

5

Wind the hackles around the base of the calf wing and tie off. Finally, dub on a small amount of muskrat fur and by lifting up the hackle fibres, wind the fur-laden thread up towards the eye. Finish the fly with a whip finish and varnish the head.

Pheasant Tail

As its name suggests, this fly is made from the tail feathers of the versatile cock Pheasant. This pattern is a popular fly in the British West Country. It is usually tied as a dry pattern (as depicted here) but quite often it is fished as a wet fly. Indeed, it is quite usual to start fishing the pattern as a dry fly and, when it becomes waterlogged, to continue to fish it as a wet fly. This pattern is attributed to Skues.

Hook: *Up-eyed 12-16*
Thread: *Pre-waxed orange*
Tail: *Honey or rusty dun cock-hackle fibres*
Body: *Cock Pheasant tail*
Rib: *Fine gold wire*
Hackle: *Honey or rusty dun*
Head: *Orange*

By altering the colour of the tail and the hackle a whole series of effective Pheasant Tail flies can be tied, such as Natural Red, Olive, Ginger, Grizzle, Grey, and Badger.

1

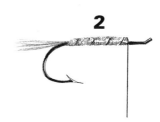

Take the thread down the shank to the bend and tie in the honey cock-hackle fibres for the tail. At the same place tie in a length of the fine gold wire for the rib and a few fibres of the cock Pheasant tail.

2

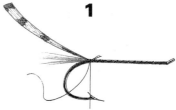

Return the thread up the shank and follow it with the Pheasant tail and then the fine gold wire. Tie off and cut away any surplus material.

3

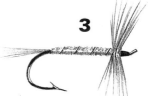

Wind on a honey or rusty dun hackle and finish the fly in the usual way.

Pink Lady

This pattern is a winged trout-fly version of the famous La Branche salmon dry fly. I have used it with great effect in the evening on still water.

Hook: *Up-eyed 8-12*
Thread: *Pre-waxed light brown or black*
Tail: *Pale-ginger cock-hackle fibres*
Body: *Pink floss silk*
Rib: *Fine oval gold tinsel*
Wing: *Starling or grey Duck in larger sizes*
Hackle: *Pale ginger*
Head: *Light brown*

1

Select matching wing slips from Starling wing quills, and, with the pinch-and-loop method, tie them in on top of the hook at the point indicated in the drawing.

2

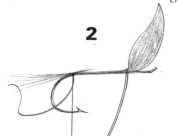

After securing the wing and setting it upright, take the thread down the shank to the bend and tie in the tail and the ribbing tinsel. Return the thread up the shank behind the wing and tie in a length of the pink floss silk.

3

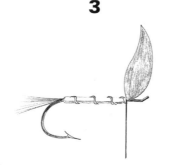

Form the body by taking the floss silk down the shank and back again. Follow this with the rib, finishing behind the wing.

4

Tie in a pale-ginger hackle behind the wing and wind on. Finish the fly in the usual way.

5

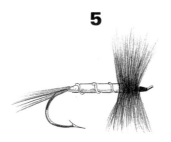

This drawing depicts the heavily hackled version used for salmon and tied on salmon dry-fly hooks.

Pope's Nondescript

One of the classic dry flies, this was devised by W.H. Pope of Dorchester. It is reckoned to be a good imitation of the Green Midge. A very good pattern on fast, broken waters.

Hook: *Up-eyed 12-16*
Thread: *Pre-waxed brown*
Tail: *Natural-red cock hackle fibres*
Body: *Light-green floss silk*
Rib: *Fine flat gold tinsel*
Wing: *Starling*
Hackle: *Natural-red cock hackle*
Head: *Brown*

Follow the instructions for such dry flies as Greenwell's Glory (page 51) and substitute with the appropriate materials.

Red Tag

This traditional fly is used for both trout and grayling, but it is as a grayling fly that it really excels. It is a very basic pattern of long lineage. When it is tied in tandem, it becomes the multi-hook lure, the Wormfly.

Hook: *Up-eyed 10-16*
Thread: *Brown or black*
Body: *Bronze Peacock herl*
Hackle: *Red Game Cock (natural red hen if you tie it as a wet fly)*
Head: *Brown or black*

This fly is tied in exactly the same way as Eric's Beetle (page 47).

Straddle Bug Mayfly

This form of mayfly dressing is extremely common in Ireland, where there are a number of mayfly dressings tied in this style. It is the type of fly that can be fished both on or beneath the surface. This was a favoured pattern of Skues.

Hook: *Down-eyed 8-10 long shank*
Thread: *Pre-waxed brown*
Tail: *Three fibres of cock Pheasant tail*
Body: *Yellow or pale-green floss silk*
Rib: *Fine oval silver tinsel*
Hackle: *Two: the first hot orange, the second Mallard breast dyed olive*
Head: *Peacock herl*

1

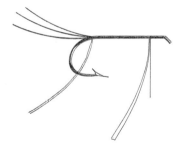

Take the thread down the shank to the bend and tie in three cock Pheasant tail fibres for the tail. At the same point tie in a length of fine oval silver tinsel. Return the thread back along the shank and tie in the floss silk for the body.

2

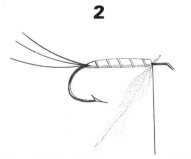

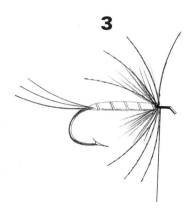

STRADDLE BUG MAYFLY

Form the body by winding the floss silk down the shank and back. Tie off and remove any surplus. Now rib the fly with the silver tinsel, tie off and remove any surplus.

3

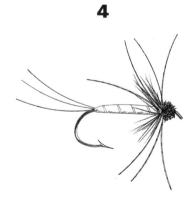

Wind on the orange hackle. Follow this with the second hackle of Mallard breast dyed olive.

4

Tie in a strand of Peacock herl and wind on to form the head. Finish the fly in the usual way.

Terry's Terror

The fly was devised by Ernest Lock and Dr Cecil Terry, and it was popularized by the well-known Eastbourne flytier Peter Deane. It is at home on both chalk stream and still water. With its rather bright tail, it must be classed as an attractor fly and is normally fished dry.

Hook: *Up-eyed 10-14*
Thread: *Brown*
Tail: *Mixed orange and yellow goat's hair*
Body: *Bronze Peacock herl*
Rib: *Fine flat copper tinsel*
Hackle: *Medium-red Game Cock*
Head: *Brown*

This simple dry fly is tied exactly the same way as the Eric's Beetle (page 47).

Tricolore

One of the best-known French dry flies for both trout and grayling, the Tricolore was developed by the famous flytier, Charles Ragot. While the original pattern had a front hackle of badger cock, it is more usual to find the version given here, which has a black hackle. This pattern was a favourite fly of the great French angler, Charles Ritz.

Hook: *Down- or up-eyed 12-16*
Thread: *Pre-waxed black*
Tail: *Ginger cock-hackle fibres*
Body: *The tying thread*
Hackles: *Three: rear blue dun, middle ginger, front black*
Head: *Black*

This fly is very similar to other palmered flies given in such as the Doobry, but it uses three hackles.

1

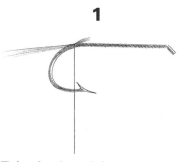

Take the thread down the shank to the bend and tie in a few fibres of ginger cock-hackle for the tail.

2

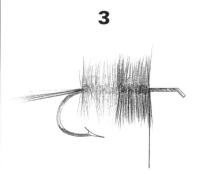

Wind on a blue-dun hackle, palmer-fashion one-third of the way up the hook. Tie off and remove any surplus feather fibre.

3

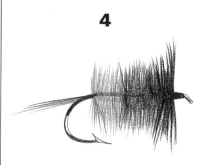

Tie in and palmer a ginger hackle for the next third of the hook.

4

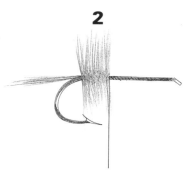

Finish off the last third with a black cock hackle and complete the fly with a neat head, whip finish, and varnish.

Walker's Red Sedge

One of the best-known patterns created by the late Richard Walker, this was originally tied on a long-shank hook. I have used this on a normal-shank size 10 hook to great effect. It should be fished quickly and skated across the surface by lifting the rod and drawing the line in, with long steady pulls. The retrieve must be constant.

Hook: *Up-eyed size 10 normal shank (can be tied on a long shank)*
Thread: *Brown*
Butt: *Fluorescent orange wool or silk*
Body: *Dark-red cock Pheasant centre-tail fibres*
Wing: *A bunch of natural-red cock-hackle fibres*
Hackle: *Two natural-red cock hackles*
Head: *Brown*

1

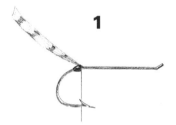

Take the thread down the hook to the bend and tie in a length of the fluorescent wool. Form a butt, tie off, and remove any surplus wool. Tie in a few fibres of dark-red cock Pheasant tail for the body. Return the thread up the shank.

2

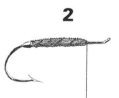

Wind the cock Pheasant tail up the shank to form the body. Tie off and cut off any surplus feather fibres.

3

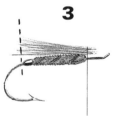

Tie in a bunch of the natural-red cock-hackle fibres on top of the hook for the wing and trim the ends straight at the tail end.

4

Wind on the two natural-red cock hackles and finish the fly in the usual way.

Welsh Partridge

This fly was the creation of the late Courtney Williams' father. The dressing was given in Courtney Williams' famous *Dictionary of Trout Flies*. The pattern is extremely versatile and it can be used wet or dry. It is generally used as an imitation of the March Brown and other largish dark mayflies. As its name suggests it has always been a useful pattern for the waters in the Principality of Wales, but its fame has spread far and wide.

Hook: *Down-eyed 10-14*
Thread: *Pre-waxed black*
Tail: *Partridge hackle fibres*
Body: *Dark-claret seal's fur or substitute*
Rib: *Fine gold tinsel*
Hackle: *Claret cock hackle with brown Partridge hackle at the front*
Head: *Black*

1

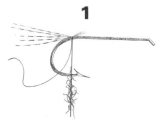

Take the thread down the shank to the bend and there tie in the Partridge hackle fibres for the tail. At the same place tie in a length of fine gold tinsel for the rib. Dub the claret seal's fur onto the tying thread.

2

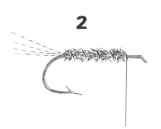

Take the fur-laden thread back along the shank to form the body. Follow this with the rib, secure, and cut away any surplus tinsel.

3

Tie in a claret cock hackle.

4

Finish with a brown Partridge hackle between the claret cock hackle and the eye. Form a neat head and complete the fly in the usual way.

Willow Fly

The Willow Fly (*Leuctra genicu-lata*) is one of the most common of the British species of stonefly (*Plecoptera*). It is abundant in the North and West of England and is one of the few stoneflies found on some of the chalk streams. The pattern given is based on the artificial devised by that great angler G.E.M. Skues.

Hook: *Up-eyed 14-16*
Thread: *Pre-waxed orange*
Body: *Mole's fur*
Hackle: *Rusty dun cock (see note)*
Wing: *Hen Blackbird (can be tied upright or spent)*
Head: *Orange*

Follow the instructions for the Olive Dun (page 61) or the Greenwells Glory (page 51) and substitute the appropriate materials.

Rusty Dun
The rusty dun shade of feather is quite rare these days. It is basically a dark-blue dun spattered with red or ginger. A reasonable substitute can be achieved by marking a dark-blue dun with a brown waterproof pen. When wound on the hook it looks just like the real thing.

Witch

Even though it is about one hundred years old, this pattern is still an excellent fly for the grayling, the "grey lady of the streams". It was created by H. A. Rolt and given in his book *Grayling Fishing in South Country Streams*. There are a number of other patterns using the name Witch and all of them are used for grayling: White Witch, Silver & Gold Witch, and the fly created by Roger Wooley, Grayling Witch.

Hook: *Up-eyed 14-16*
Thread: *Pre-waxed light brown (sherry spinner)*
Tail: *Red floss silk*
Body: *Green Peacock sword herl*
Rib: *Fine flat silver tinsel*
Hackle: *Honey-dun or blue-dun cock hackle*
Head: *Brown*

Follow the instructions for any of the palmered flies (see Bibio, page 74) and substitute the appropriate materials given above.

COCH-Y-BONDHU

Yorke's Favourite

This is a pattern used on Trawsfynydd Lake in North Wales. It was named after a gentleman who travelled the North Wales area selling flies. It is used when the Heather Fly is on the water (see the Hawthorn, page 54).

Hook: *Down-eyed 10-12*
Thread: *Pre-waxed black*
Tail: *Scarlet Goose (Red Ibis substitute)*
Body: *Black Ostrich herl*
Hackle: *Coch-y-Bondhu (dark furnace)*
Head: *Black*

Follow the instructions for Eric's Beetle (page 47) and substitute the appropriate materials.

Dapping Flies

Taking trout and sea trout on the dap is one of the most exciting methods of fishing from a boat. Dapping flies must be good floaters, so they are generally heavily hackled. The Loch Ordie pattern already given (page 59) is such a fly. The two flies that follow are traditional Scottish dapping patterns. Artificials and naturals of mayflies, craneflies, and even grasshoppers are often used for dapping.

Dapping has long been a very exciting and on the right day (if the wind is favourable) an extremely successful way of catching fish. You need a rod that is light and up to 5 m (15') in length. The heavily palmered flies that I have depicted show how substantial they can be. The dapping fly should be well waterproofed with one of the excellent prod-ucts that are on the market. Personally I have always used Per-maflote with great success.

The dapping fly is required to be just airborne in front of our drifting boat and literally needs to dance on the water. The main drawback with dapping, apart from the occasional heart stopping moments that occur as trout and salmon boil on the lake, is that there are many missed fish as we react too quickly and strike too soon. Dapping needs a fraction of a delay with the strike.

Coch-y-Bondhu
Hook: *Up-eyed dry-fly salmon hook*
Thread: *Pre-waxed black*
Tag: *Flat silver or gold tinsel*
Hackle: *Heavily palmered furnace hackle*
Head: *Black*

BADGER

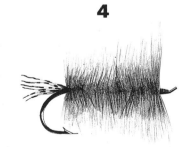

Palmer the hackles right up the shank and complete the fly in the usual way.

4

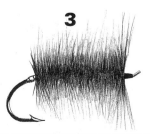

The second fly is tied up in the same way except that, instead of a tinsel tag, a few fibres of Guinea Fowl are tied in to form a tail.

Badger

Hook: *Up-eyed dry-fly salmon hook*
Thread: *Pre-waxed black*
Tail: *Black-and-white Guinea Fowl or grizzle hackle fibres*
Hackle: *Heavily palmered badger hackle*
Head: *Black*

2

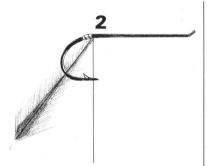

Form the tag, secure, and cut off any spare material. Tie in a furnace hackle by its tip. Larger-size hooks may require two hackles, and further hackles may be required if the fly to be imitated is large.

1

Take the thread down the shank to the bend and tie in a strip of flat tinsel for the tag.

Troutbeck Lake, at an altitude of 7,000 feet, is in the Eastern Highlands of Zimbabwe. The trout fishing in the lake and in the surrounding rivers is superb.

III
WET
FLIES

Adult Buzzer

The Chironomid midge known by the name buzzer by most of today's anglers is perhaps the most important item of diet for still-water trout. Many species are also found in rivers. Although trout mainly feed on the pupae of the midge they often rise to the surface to take the adult fly. This pattern is as good as any to represent this stage in the life cycle of the Chironomid midge. It can be tied in a number of different colours, for instance: black, brown, olive, green, or ginger. The fly depicted is the ginger version.

Hook: *Sedge-style hook 10-16*
Thread: *Pre-waxed orange*
Abdomen: *Hot-orange Swan or Goose herl*
Rib: *Stripped Peacock herl dyed ginger*
Thorax: *Beige/brown fur*
Back of Thorax: *Hen (secondary wing quill) dyed ginger/orange*
Wing: *Light-blue dun hackle points*
Hackle: *Ginger or honey cock*
Head: *Orange*

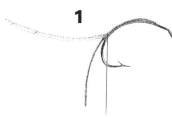

1

Take the thread about one-third of the way along the shank and tie in (pointing rearwards) stripped and dyed Peacock herl. Continue the thread down the shank and around the bend, tying in the stripped herl as you go along. Tying in the rib at this point helps to prevent an unsightly bulge at the bend of the hook. Now tie in a portion of the hot-orange Swan or Goose herl for the abdomen.

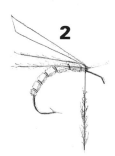

2

Return the thread back along the shank to where you tied in the stripped Peacock herl for the rib. Follow the thread by winding the Swan or Goose herl around the hook. Follow this with the rib. Secure and cut off any surplus

fibre. The abdomen is now formed. Tie in a piece of ginger orange hen-feather fibre for the back of the thorax, and on either side tie in two light-blue dun hackle points for the wing. Dub the thread with some beige/brown fur to form the thorax.

3

Wind on the thorax and then tie in a ginger or honey cock hackle.

4

Take the thorax-back feather over the thorax and secure. Remove any surplus feather. Most of the hackle fibres are forced beneath the hook to simulate the legs. Complete the fly with the usual whip finish and varnish.

Bibio

A fly of Irish origin, Bibio is now popular with reservoir fishermen throughout the British Isles. It is used in the main as a bob fly in a team of three flies when fishing in the traditional loch style. A popular fly for the great limestone lakes of Ireland such as Lough Corrib and Lough Mask.

Hook: *Down-eyed 8-12*
Thread: *Black*
Body: *Black seal's fur and red seal's fur or substitute*
Rib: *Fine oval silver tinsel*
Hackle: *Palmered black cock, with two turns at the shoulder*
Head: *Black*

1

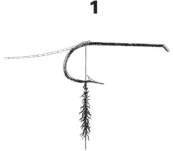

Take the thread down the shank to the bend and tie in a length of the fine oval silver tinsel for the rib. Dub a small amount of the black seal's fur onto the thread.

2

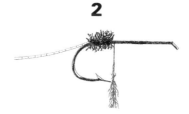

Take the fur-laden thread a third of the way up the shank and remove any surplus black fur. Dub a small amount of red seal's fur onto the thread.

3

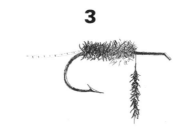

Wind the red seal's fur onto the next third of the shank, then dub some more black fur onto the thread.

4

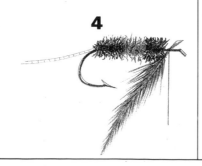

Complete the body with the black fur and tie in a black cock hackle.

5

Palmer the hackle down the body and secure with the fine oval silver tinsel.

6

Wind the tinsel back along the shank to form the rib and finish the fly in the usual way.

Blae & Silver

The "Blae" series of flies have long been favourites with both Scottish and English lake fishermen. Perhaps the best known of the series is the Blae & Black. The Blae & Silver is often used as a point fly in a team of three in traditional loch-style fishing. The word Blae is an old Scottish word meaning blue, to be precise, a light greyish blue as found in the feathers used for the wings of this series of flies, from the Mallard or Starling. This pattern is also used for sea trout.

Hook: *Down-eyed 8-14*
Thread: *Pre-waxed black*
Tail: *Golden Pheasant tippet*
Body: *Flat silver tinsel, Mylar, or Lurex*
Rib: *Silver wire or fine oval silver tinsel*
Hackle: *Ginger cock hackle (sometimes badger is used)*
Wing: *Grey Mallard (Starling wing quill in smaller sizes)*
Head: *Black*

1

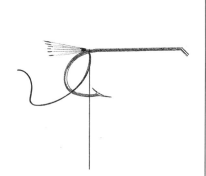

Take the thread down the shank to the bend and tie in a few fibres of Golden Pheasant tippet for the tail. At the same place tie in a length of silver wire or fine oval silver tinsel for the rib.

2

Return the thread up the shank and there tie in a length of flat silver tinsel, Mylar, or Lurex for the body.

3

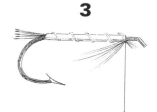

Take the body material down the shank, wind the rib material over this, secure, and cut off any surplus. Beneath the hook tie in a bunch of ginger cock hackle fibres for the hackle.

4

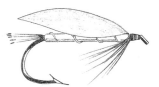

Tie a matching pair of grey Mallard wing slips on top of the hook. Complete the fly with the usual whip finish and varnish.

Blue Zulu

A number of anglers have not found this Zulu variant as successful as the original, but I find it a useful pattern to include in a team of wet flies, especially on bright days. I have also used it successfully on migratory trout.

Hook: *Down-eyed 8-12*
Thread: *Black*
Tail: *A tuft of bright scarlet wool*
Body: *Black seal's fur or substitute*
Rib: *Flat silver tinsel*
Hackle: *Blue cock hackle*
Head: *Black*

Tie the fly in the same way as the Bibio (opposite), but this time there is a single body colour, which makes the tying slightly easier.

Bradshaw's Fancy

This fly was created by Henry Bradshaw of Leeds. Though over a century old, it is considered to be a fine grayling pattern by many of today's anglers.

Hook: *Down-eyed 14-16*
Thread: *Dark purple*
Tail: *Crimson silk or wool*
Body: *Bronze Peacock herl with crimson silk or wool*
Hackle: *Norwegian Crow neck (a blue-dun hen will substitute)*
Head: *Dark purple*

1

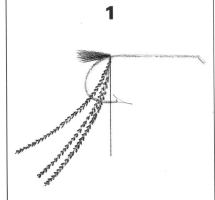

Take the thread down the shank to the bend and tie in a tuft of crimson wool or silk for the tail. At the same place tie in a few bronze Peacock herls for the body.

2

Form a rope with the Peacock herl and the tying thread, wind it up the shank to the point shown, and there tie in another length of crimson silk or wool.

3

Wind on the crimson silk or wool as a collar. Tie in and wind on the hackle of Norwegian Crow neck or blue-dun hen. Finish the fly in the usual way.

Brown Spider

Spider-dressed flies are among the earliest fishing patterns used on rivers. This particular one is used with some success on still water, where it can represent a wide variety of aquatic creatures. It is closely allied to the well-known still-water fly, the Black & Peacock.

All spider patterns can be tied in this way. Although they are among the easiest to tie, spiders are considered to be some of the most effective fish-catching flies of all.

Hook: *Down-eyed 10-14*
Thread: *Light brown*
Body: *Bronze Peacock herl*
Hackle: *Brown Partridge*
Head: *Light brown*

1

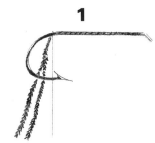

Take the thread down the hook to the bend and there tie in two or three strands of bronze Peacock herl.

2

Twist the herl into a rope along with the tying thread.

3

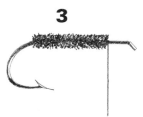

Return the herl-laden thread up the shank to form the body. Tie off and remove any surplus herl.

4

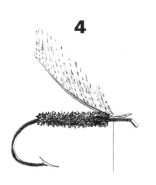

Select a brown Partridge back feather for the hackle, which, because you want it to be fairly sparse, must be stripped of flue from one side. Tie in on top of the hook by the tip, not the stalk.

5

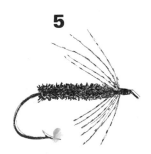

Wind on the hackle, tie off, and remove the rest of the hackle. Form a small neat head, whip finish, and varnish.

Cardinal

It is doubtful if this fly is tied to represent the Cardinal Beetle, although I must admit that I have only found this insect in close proximity to water. We can assume that this fly is a pure attractor pattern. It is useful when trout are feeding upon bloodworms.

Hook: *Down-eyed 8-12*
Thread: *Pre-waxed red*
Tail: *Red Ibis substitute (e.g. dyed Goose)*
Body: *Scarlet floss silk*
Rib: *Fine gold wire*
Hackle: *Scarlet cock*
Wing: *Red Ibis substitute (e.g. dyed Goose)*
Head: *Red*

1

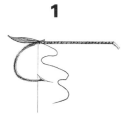

Take the thread down the shank to the bend and tie in a strip of the Red Ibis substitute for the tail. Tie in a length of fine gold wire for the rib.

2

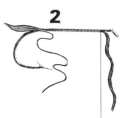

Return the thread back up the shank and there tie in a length of scarlet floss silk.

3

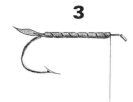

Form the body by winding the scarlet floss silk down the shank and back again. Secure and remove any surplus. Rib the body with the fine gold wire.

4

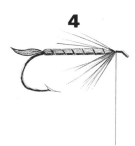

Wind on the scarlet cock hackle, or tie in a bunch of scarlet cock-hackle fibres beneath the hook.

5

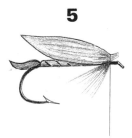

Use the pinch-and-loop method to tie in a matched pair of Red Ibis substitute wing slips on top of the hook.

6

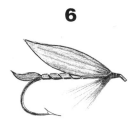

Finish the fly with a whip finish and varnish.

Cock Robin

This pattern hails from the Emerald Isle and is one of the traditional Mallard series of wet flies (a series that includes such favourites as the Mallard & Claret and Mallard & Gold). This particular pattern is also called the Mallard & Mixed or the Jointed Mallard because of its bi-coloured body. It is effective for both trout and sea trout.

Hook: *Down-eyed 8-12*
Thread: *Pre-waxed black*
Tail: *Bronze Mallard fibres*
Body: *In two halves; rear end: golden-olive seal's fur; front end: red seal's fur (or substitutes)*
Rib: *Fine oval gold tinsel*
Hackle: *Natural-red cock hackle*
Wing: *Bronze Mallard flank*
Head: *Black*

1

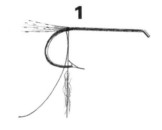

Take the thread down the shank to the bend and tie in a few fibres of bronze Mallard for the tail. At the same place tie in a length of fine oval gold tinsel. Now dub the tying thread with enough golden-olive seal's fur to make the rear end of the body.

2

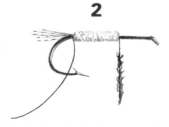

Wind the fur-laden thread halfway down the shank. Onto the rest of the tying thread dub the red seal's fur.

3

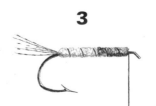

Wind the thread with the red fur down the shank to complete the body. Follow this with the fine oval gold tinsel, tie off, and cut off any surplus tinsel.

4

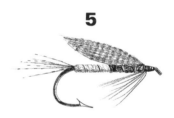

Tie under the hook a bunch of natural-red cock-hackle fibres for the hackle.

5

Tie slips of bronze Mallard on top of the hook to form the wing (see below). Complete the fly in the usual way.

Soft feather wings

First treat the feathers with a spray of "Artist's Fixative". This is available from all artist supplies shops. Having fixed the feathers, cut two slips about 8 mm (5/16") wide from the left-sided feather and two slips from the right. If only one slip is used, the wing will look a little thin and scrawny. Offer these slips to the top of the hook with the pinch-and-loop method.

Col. Downman's Fancy

A number of fancy attractor patterns have used the bright blue barred feathers found on a Jay's wing. I believe the fly was first used on the Scottish lochs. This pattern was given by John Veniard in his book *Lake and Reservoir Flies*.

Hook: *Down-eyed 8 10*
Thread: *Pre-waxed black*
Tail: *Teal flank fibres*
Body: *Black floss silk*
Rib: *Fine oval silver tinsel*
Hackle: *Black hen*
Wing: *Barred blue Jay wing feather*
Cheek: *Jungle Cock or substitute*
Head: *Black*

1

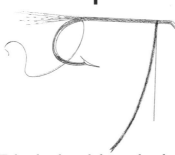

Take the thread down the shank to the bend and tie in the Teal flank fibres. At the same place tie in a length of the fine oval silver tinsel for the rib. Return the thread back along the shank and there tie in a length of the black floss silk.

2

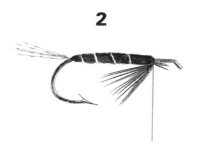

Form the body by winding the black floss silk down the shank and back again. Follow this with

even turns of the fine oval silver tinsel. Secure and cut off any surplus floss or tinsel. Tie in a bunch of black hen-hackle fibres beneath the hook.

3

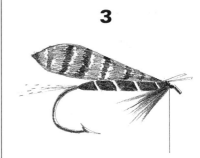

Place two blue-barred Jay feathers back-to-back and tie in on top of the hook.

4

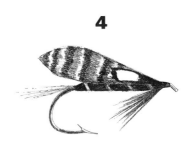

Flank the wing with two Jungle Cock feathers and finish the fly in the usual way.

Dark Spanish Needle

This is one of the traditional wet spider patterns created by T. E. Pritt, author of the classic *Yorkshire Trout Flies*, 1885. It is sometimes known simply as the Needle Fly or the Dark Needle. It is an imitation of the natural Stonefly *(Leuctra fusca)*.

Hook: *Down-eyed 14-16*
Thread: *Pre-waxed orange*
Body: *Orange floss silk*
Hackle: *Dark brown feather from an Owl's wing*
Head: *Peacock herl*

2

Return the thread back up the shank and follow this with the orange floss silk in order to form the body. Select a dark-brown hackle from an Owl's wing (or use a substitute such as a Grouse's body feather) and strip all the flues from one side of the feather. Tie this half hackle on top of the hook.

Delphi

This is another sea-trout fly that is sometimes used for lake trout. One of the early versions of this pattern also sported a wing of barred Teal flank. The fly is named for the famous Delphi waters in the Ballinskill fishery district in western Ireland.

Hook: *Down-eyed 6-8*
Thread: *Pre-waxed black*
Tail: *Two Jungle Cock feathers*
Body: *Flat silver tinsel or Lurex*
Rib: *Fine silver wire*
Hackle: *Black cock*
Head: *Black*

1

Take the thread down the shank to the bend. Tie in a length of orange floss silk (or you can form the body by just using the tying thread).

3

Wind on the hackle two or three turns at the most (stripping off one side guarantees a sparse hackle). Tie off, remove any surplus feather, and then form a head with a strand of Peacock herl. Complete the fly in the usual manner.

1

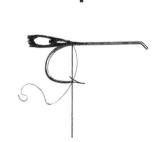

Take the thread down the shank to the bend and tie in two Jungle Cock feathers tied back-to-back. At the same point tie in a length of fine silver wire.

2

Return the thread half way up the shank and there tie in a length of flat silver tinsel or Lurex.

3

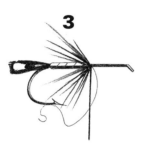

Take the tinsel or Lurex down the hook and back, and follow this with the fine silver wire. Trim away any surplus tinsel. Tie in a black cock hackle. Tie it off and cut away any surplus feather. Tie in another length of fine silver wire, also in the middle of the shank. Don't cut off the thread.

4

Take the thread to the eye of the hook where you tie in another length of flat silver tinsel or Lurex. Complete the rest of the body as in Step 3. Follow up with the fine silver wire and add the second black hackle. Finish the fly in the usual way.

Doobry

A fly from the Orkneys, first tied in 1980 by Stan Headley.

Hook: *Down-eyed 8-12*
Thread: *Pre-waxed black*
Tail: *Fluorescent scarlet wool or orange/red (No 5 Datum Glowbright Series) tied short*
Body: *Flat gold tinsel*
Rib: *Gold wire*
Hackles: *Palmered black cock fronted by hot orange*
Head: *Black*

1

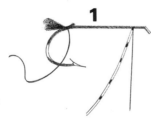

Take the thread down the shank to the bend and tie in a tuft of fluorescent scarlet wool and a length of gold wire. Return the thread along the shank and tie in a length of flat gold tinsel.

2

Form the body by taking the tinsel down the shank and back again, tie off, and cut away any surplus. Tie in a black cock hackle by the stalk.

3

Palmer the hackle down to the bend and secure with the gold wire for the ribbing. Then take the gold wire up the body, securing the hackle as you go along and taking care not to trap too many fibres. (Trapped fibres can be released afterwards with a dubbing needle.) Remove the tip of the hackle left at the end.

4

Wind on a hot-orange cock hackle at the front and finish the fly in the usual manner.

Extractor

This fly was devised by the well-known firm of Rogans in Bally-shannon, Ireland. It is sometimes given the name of Rogans' Extractor. It is a fancy lake pattern.

Hook: *Down-eyed 8-12*
Thread: *Pre-waxed black*
Tail: *Red Golden Pheasant body feather fibres*
Body: *Flat gold tinsel*
Rib: *Gold wire*
Hackle: *Lemon yellow with Golden Pheasant body feather fibres in front (tied beneath the hook)*
Wing: *Bronze Mallard*
Head: *Black*

Follow the instructions for the Gold Butcher (page 84) and use the method involving the soft feather wing (see note on page 78).

February Red

The February Red (*Taeniopteryx nebulosa*) is one of the early emerging stoneflies found on British North Country rivers from February to April. This is a traditional wet-winged pattern.

Hook: *Down-eyed 12-16*
Thread: *Pre-waxed black*
Body: *Reddish claret mohair at the tail end, followed by brown mohair.*
Wing: *Speckled hen wing*
Hackle: *Dark-grizzle hen or cock*
Head: *Black*

1

Take the thread down the shank to the bend and there dub on some reddish claret mohair.

2

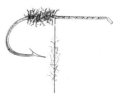

Wind on the fur-laden thread to the point shown to form a butt, then dub on some brown mohair.

3

Complete the body with the brown mohair and tie in a bunch of dark-grizzle hackle fibres beneath the hook.

4

Tie on top of the hook a pair of speckled hen-wing slips using the pinch-and-loop method. Finish the fly in the usual way.

Fenian

The Fenians were the legendary band of followers of Finn Mac-Cool, famed in Irish folk tales. This fly is a typical Irish lake pattern. The Irish national colours are to be found in the body of the fly.

Hook: *Down-eyed 8-12*
Thread: *Pre-waxed black*
Tail: *Golden Pheasant crest*
Tip: *Oval silver tinsel*
Body: *Rear third yellow-orange floss silk, front two-thirds emerald-green floss silk*
Rib: *Oval gold or silver tinsel*
Hackle: *Yellow cock*
Wing: *Bronze Mallard*
Head: *Black*

1

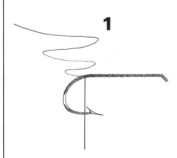

Take the thread down the shank to the bend and there tie in a length of oval tinsel for the tip.

2

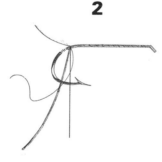

Wind on the tinsel to form the tip, and then tie in the Golden Pheasant crest for the tail, the ribbing tinsel, and a length of yellow-orang floss silk for the rear third of the body.

3

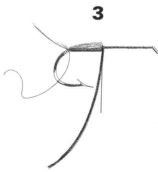

Take the thread one-third of the way up the shank and follow with the yellow-orange floss silk, secure, and cut off any surplus. Tie in the emerald-green floss silk.

4

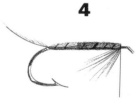

Take the tying thread back along the shank and finish the body by winding on the emerald-green floss silk. Follow this with the ribbing tinsel. Underneath the hook tie in some yellow cock hackle fibres.

5

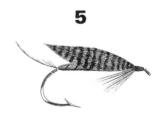

Tie on the bronze Mallard wing and complete the fly in the usual way.

Gold Butcher

The original Butcher had a silver body, but this variant is tied, as its name suggests, with gold tinsel. Many anglers prefer the gold version, especially for sea trout.

Hook: *Down-eyed 8-12*
Thread: *Pre-waxed black*
Tail: *Red Ibis substitute* (e.g. dyed Goose)
Body: *Flat gold tinsel (Mylar or Lurex)*
Rib: *Fine oval gold tinsel*
Hackle: *Black cock or hen*
Wing: *Blue Mallard*
Head: *Black*

1

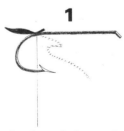

Take the thread down the shank to the bend and tie in the tail feather slip. At the same point tie in a length of the fine oval gold tinsel for the rib.

2

Return the thread back along the shank and tie in a length of the flat gold tinsel for the body.

3

Take the flat gold tinsel down the shank and back again. Secure and cut off the surplus. Now wind the fine oval gold tinsel for the rib up the shank, tie off, and cut off any surplus.

4

Tie in a bunch of black cock- or hen-hackle fibres beneath the hook.

5

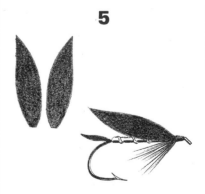

Select two equal left and right feather slips from a blue Mallard wing quill. Tie them in on top of the hook. Complete the fly in the usual manner.

Golden Olive

Another fly from the "Emerald Isle", this is used on the famous limestone loughs. It is most likely that the fish take this pattern for a hatching sedge. There are many anglers who swear by it as a sea-trout pattern too. There are a number of dressings for this fly. The one given is as good as any.

Hook: *Down-eyed 8-12*
Thread: *Olive*
Tail: *Golden Pheasant crest*
Tag *(optional)*: *Orange floss silk*
Body: *Golden-olive seal's fur or substitute*
Rib: *Fine oval gold tinsel*
Hackle: *Golden-olive cock*
Wing: *Bronze Mallard*
Head: *Olive*

The method of tying is the same as for the Fiery Brown (page 143). Apart from the tail, all the other steps are the same.

Golden Olive Bumble

The original "bumble"-dressed flies were allegedly fished in the county of Derbyshire. They are tied in a variety of shades and colours. This particular pattern was created by T. C. Kingsmill-Moore, whose book *A Man May Fish* has become a classic of modern fly fishing. The Golden Olive Bumble was perhaps his most favoured pattern, the colouration of which is taken from the well-known standard pattern, the Invicta. Tied as it is with a double palmered hackle, the Golden Olive Bumble resembles an insect such as a sedge struggling in the surface film. All the "bumble" patterns can be fished wet or dry, and they make an ideal fly for the top dropper in a team of flies.

Hook: *Down-eyed 8-12*
Thread: *Brown*
Tail: *Golden Pheasant crest*
Body: *Golden olive seal's fur or substitute*
Rib: *Oval gold tinsel*
Hackles: *One palmered golden-olive and one natural-red cock*
Front Hackle: *Blue Jay or dyed blue Guinea Fowl*
Head: *Brown*

1

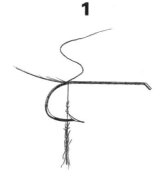

Take the thread down the hook to the bend and tie in the Golden Pheasant crest for the tail and a strand of oval gold tinsel for the rib. Dub the thread with golden-olive seal's fur.

2

Take the fur-laden thread back up the shank and there tie in the cock hackles, the golden-olive and the natural-red.

3

Tie them in with the stalks close together. Wind the two hackles down the shank together. To do this, grip the tips firmly in the hackle pliers, keep taut, and wind down to the bend of the hook, allowing the two colours to intermingle.

4

If the blue Jay feather is chosen, you must first prepare it, because its stalk is a little stiff and thick. With a scalpel or razor blade split the stalk down the middle and discard the non-coloured side.

5

Tie the blue side in by the tip on top of the hook and wind on in the normal way.

If you use a dyed-blue Guinea Fowl feather treat it as a normal hackle and tie also by the tip.

Complete the fly with a small head, whip finish, and varnish.

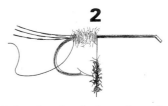

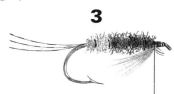

Grenadier

This fly was created by the late Dr Bell, who also tied the famous Amber nymphs for fishing Blagdon Water. This fly continues to catch fish wherever it is used. I have found it most useful when the trout are feeding on *Daphnia*.

Hook: *Down-eyed 10-16*
Thread: *Pre-waxed sherry-spinner colour or orange*
Body: *Orange seal's fur or floss silk*
Hackle: *Two turns of light-furnace cock*
Head: *Brown or orange*

This fly is a simple, hackled wet pattern. Follow the instructions for other spider-type wet flies (such as the Brown Spider on page 76) and substitute with the materials given above.

Grey Monkey

This pattern is a traditional Irish lake fly. Larger versions were tied for salmon. The original fur used was as, the name suggests, monkey fur. It is more usual these days to use a grey seal's fur substitute.

Hook: *Down-eyed 8-12*
Thread: *Pre-waxed black*
Tail: *Teal tail fibres*
Body: *In two parts: rear third golden olive seal's fur; front two-thirds grey seal's fur (or substitutes)*
Rib: *Oval gold tinsel*
Hackle: *Grey*
Wing: *Starling or grey Duck in larger sizes*
Cheek (optional): *Jungle Cock*
Head: *Black*

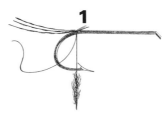

1

Take the thread down the shank to the bend and tie in the Teal tail fibres. Tie in a length of the oval gold tinsel for the rib and dub some golden-olive fur onto the thread.

2

Take the fur-laden thread one-third of the way up the shank, and then dub the thread with the grey seal's fur.

3

Complete the body by taking the grey-fur-dubbed thread up the shank. Follow this with the rib. Secure and cut off any surplus. Tie in a bunch of grey hackle fibres beneath the hook.

4

Tie two slips of Starling or Duck on top of the hook and, when secured, tie in a Jungle Cock feather on either side. Finish with the usual whip finish and varnish.

Hardy's Favourite

This fly was created by J.J. Hardy of the famous tackle firm of Alnwick and Pall Mall, London. The fly is especially popular in Scotland.

Hook: *Down-eyed 10-14*
Thread: *Pre-waxed black*
Body: *Claret floss silk or seal's fur*
Rib: *A strand of Peacock herl*
Hackle: *Grey Partridge*
Wing: *Woodcock*

Tie up using the standard wet fly method (see Cock Robin, page 78).

Haul a Gwynt

The translation of the Welsh *Haul a Gwynt* is "Sun and Wind" and, as its name suggests, it is a good fly to use when still-water fishing under such conditions. It is a pattern from North Wales, where it is highly popular on such waters as Trawsfynydd Lake and Llyn Brenig reservoir.

Hook: *Down-eyed 10-14*
Thread: *Pre-waxed black*
Body: *Black Ostrich herl*
Wing: *Crow (sometimes Snipe is used)*
Hackle: *Black-tipped cock Pheasant neck*
Head: *Black*

1

Take the thread down the shank to the bend and there tie in a couple of strands of Ostrich herl.

2

Return the thread back along the shank and follow with the Ostrich herl, tying a nice plump body.

3

The next stage is the wing (not the hackle), so tie in two matching slips of Crow or Snipe wing quill.

4

Tie in the hackle and finish the fly in the usual way.

Kate McLaren

A Scottish loch fly dating back to the 1930s, it was created by William Robertson. It is usually fished as the "bob" fly in a team of wet flies in the traditional loch-style fishing. In recent years, it has become popular in other parts of the world.

Hook: *Down-eyed 8-12*
Thread: *Black*
Tail: *Golden Pheasant crest*
Body: *Black seal's fur or substitute*
Rib: *Oval silver tinsel*
Hackle: *Palmered black cock, and at the head reddish-brown cock*
Head: *Black*

This fly can be tied in the same way as the Bibio (page 74), a fly which is very similar in both appearance and usage. However, the method shown below gives an alternative way of putting on the palmered hackle.

1

Take the thread down the shank and there tie in the Golden Pheasant crest. At the same place tie in a strand of oval gold tinsel and by the tip a black cock hackle. Dub some black seal's fur onto the tying thread.

2

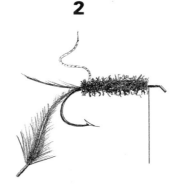

Take the fur-laden thread back up the hook shank to form the body.

3

Now palmer the hackle up the body, tie off and cut away any surplus feather.

4

Carefully wind on the gold rib, taking care not to trap too many hackle fibres (trapped fibres can be released later with a dubbing needle). Tie off the rib.

5

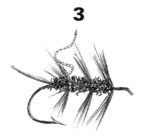

Wind on the reddish-brown hackle at the front, form a small head, and complete the fly in the usual way.

Kingsmill

Another pattern (see the Golden Olive Bumble) created by T. C. Kingsmill-Moore, for both trout and sea trout. A very popular fly on such waters as Lough Melvin in Ireland.

Hook: *Down-eyed 8-12*
Thread: *Black*
Tail: *Golden Pheasant crest*
Tag or Butt *(optional)*: *Blue floss silk*
Body: *Black Ostrich herl*
Rib: *Oval silver tinsel*
Hackle: *Black cock*
Wing: *Rook, secondary feather rolled tight*
Cheek: *Jungle Cock or substitute*
Topping: *Golden Pheasant crest to meet the tail*
Head: *Black*

1

Take the thread down the shank to the bend and tie in the Golden Pheasant crest. Tie in also a length of the oval silver tinsel for the rib and the black Ostrich herl for the body.

2

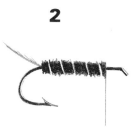

Return the thread up the shank, and follow this with the Ostrich herl and then the silver rib.

3

Tie in a black cock hackle.

4

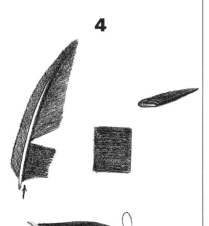

Select about one inch of Rook feather fibre and roll it up carefully, in much the same way as you would roll a carpet. Tie this wing on top of the hook by the soft loop method.

5

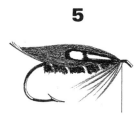

Tie in the Jungle Cock feathers on either side of the wing.

6

Tie in a Golden Pheasant crest so that it goes over the wing and meets the tail feather. Finish off with a neat head and the usual whip finish.

Mallard & Silver

Another from the Mallard series of wet flies for lake trout, this is also used for sea trout. The Mallard & Gold is another firm favourite with both the trout and the sea trout angler.

Hook: *Down-eyed 8-12*
Thread: *Pre-waxed black*
Tail: *Golden Pheasant tippet*
Body: *Flat silver tinsel*
Rib: *Oval silver tinsel*
Hackle: *Black cock or hen hackle*
Wing: *Bronze Mallard*
Head: *Black*

Follow the instructions for the Teal Green & Silver (page 98) and substitute the appropriate materials.

Malloch's Favourite

A traditional pattern that is usually fished in Scotland during
Chironomid activity.

Hook: *Down-eyed 10-14*
Thread: *Pre-waxed black*
Tail: *Natural red cock-hackle*
  fibres
Rib: *Silver wire*
Body: *Stripped Peacock quill*
Hackle: *Blue dun*
Wing: *Woodcock*
Head: *Black*

This is a standard wet-fly pattern. Follow instructions for the
Cock Robin (page 78), substituting with the above materials.

Murrough (Murragh)

The Murrough or Great Red Sedge (*Phryganae grandisor striata*) is one of the largest of the sedges found in the British Isles. The Murrough is the Irish name for this fly. There are many dressings for this particular pattern. The version given here is a wet fly.

Hook: *Down-eyed 8-10*
Thread: *Pre-waxed yellow or light brown*
Body: *Brown fur, wool, or polypropylene*
Hackle: *Brown cock hackle*
Wing: *Brown mottled hen wing quill*
Antennae: *Two cock-hackle stalks*
Head: *Brown*

1

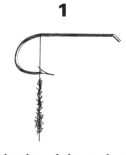

Take the thread down the shank to the bend of the hook and dub on the brown fur or substitute.

2

Take the dubbed thread back along the shank to form the body. Tie in a bunch of brown cock-hackle fibres beneath the hook.

3

Select a slip of brown mottled hen feather from a right quill and a slip from a left quill. Place them together dull side in and offer them to the top of the hook. Tie in by the pinch-and-loop method.

4

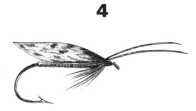

Strip two cock hackles and tie the stalks in on top of the hook, so that they project over the eye. Finish the fly in the usual way with a whip finish and varnish.

Olive Quill

This is a wet fly version of the dry pattern already given. We show it because some fishermen prefer to fish with a sub-surface fly rather than with a dry pattern. The fly is most effective in fast-flowing rivers, though some still-water anglers like to include natural-looking flies like this in a team of wet flies for the traditional loch-style fishing.

Hook: *Down-eyed 10-14*
Thread: *Pre-waxed olive*
Tail: *Olive cock or hen-hackle fibres*
Body: *Stripped Peacock herl*
Wing: *Grey Starling or Duck-wing quill slips*
Hackle: *Olive hen or soft-fibred cock hackle*
Head: *Olive*

Follow the instructions for the dry version (see page 62), using the much softer hackles. The wing on the wet fly is applied last and is tied on the top of the hook, sloping backwards.

Shredge

This pattern was created by Tony Knight as a wet fly for fishing such waters as Rutland Water. It can be considered as a broad-spectrum pattern that represents an emergent sedge. It is usually fished in the months of July and August at the height of the sedge hatches.

Hook: *Down-eyed 10-12*
Thread: *Primrose or golden olive*
Body: *A mixture of seal's fur or substitute, 70% cinnamon and 30% yellow, to give a light tobacco colour*
Rib: *Gold wire*
Hackle: *Palest ginger hen*
Wing: *Pale-grey Mallard wing quill*
Head: *Primrose or golden olive*

This fly is tied in the same way as the Fiery Brown (page 143). Follow the step-by-step instructions and substitute with the appropriate materials

Silver Doctor

The original Silver Doctor is a standard and well-proven fly for salmon. This version is a far simpler fly used in the main for sea trout. It has also been used as a lake fly. At one time it was even considered a good pattern for the steelhead of North America.

Hook: *Down-eyed 6-10*
Thread: *Pre-waxed black*
Tail: *Golden Pheasant tippet fibres*
Body: *Flat silver tinsel or Lurex*
Rib: *Oval silver tinsel*
Hackle: *Blue cock-hackle fibres*
Wing: *Strips of dyed Goose: green, yellow, and red, joined together; grey Mallard flank-feather fibres either side. Sometimes the whole wing is veiled with the Mallard feather.*
Head: *Black*

Built wings

The natural construction found in a wing-feather quill enables the flytier to take strips from a variety of different-coloured feathers and also from different wing quills, and re-combine into a solid wing once more. This is possible because of the fine hook-lets found along the edges of the barbules. The arrangement can be likened to a zip fastener or perhaps even a natural Velcro.

1

In tying flies with more complex built wings, it is always advisable to prepare a number of right and left wings prior to actually starting to tie the fly. Take strips from the left and right wing quills that have been dyed red, yellow, and green (red at the bottom, then yellow, then green). Hold them close together between thumb and forefinger and stroke them together. You will see that they combine quite easily. A gentle spray of fixative helps to keep the three strips together.

2

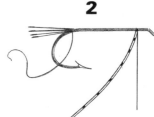

Take the tying thread down the shank to the bend and there tie in a few fibres of Golden Pheasant tippet for the tail. At the same place tie a length of the oval silver tinsel. Return the thread back up the shank and tie in a strip of the flat silver tinsel or Lurex.

3

Form the body by winding the flat silver tinsel or Lurex down the shank and back again. Now wind the oval silver tinsel up the body in even turns to form the rib. Tie in a bunch of blue cock-hackle fibres underneath the hook.

4

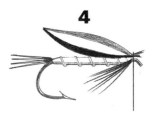

Place the built wing on top of the hook and tie in by the pinch-and-loop method. Secure and cut off any surplus feather.

5

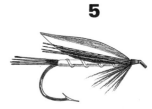

Tie in a few fibres of grey Mallard flank on either side of the hook and complete the fly with the usual whip finish and varnish

Sooty Olive

There are a number of dressings for this fly, which is popular on many of the large Irish lakes. Many of the Irish lake patterns use a tail of Golden Pheasant tippet as an extra attractor, though some fishermen believe that it emulates the shuck of the hatching Olive.

Hook: *Down-eyed 8-12*
Thread: *Pre-waxed black*
Tail: *Golden Pheasant tippet*
Body: *Dark olive fur*
Rib: *Fine gold wire*
Hackle: *Black*
Wing: *Bronze Mallard*
Head: *Black*

Follow the instructions for the Cock Robin (page 78), but with a single body colour.

Teal & Black

A traditional wet fly, this is just one of the series that uses a Teal flank feather as the wing. This pattern works well when the trout have been feeding on Chironomids. It is most popular in Scotland and in Ireland as a sea-trout fly.

Hook: *Down-eyed 8-12*
Thread: *Pre-waxed black*
Tail: *Golden Pheasant tippet*
Body: *Black seal's fur, wool, or silk*
Rib: *Fine oval tinsel*
Hackle: *Black hen or cock hackle*
Wing: *Teal flank.*
Head: *Black*

See instructions for the Teal Green & Silver (Page 98) and substitute the appropriate materials.

Teal Green & Silver

Perhaps the best-known fly from the Teal series is the Teal Blue & Silver, but this pattern, with green instead of blue, is widely used for sea trout in Ireland.

Hook: *Down-eyed 8-12*
Thread: *Pre-waxed black*
Tail: *Golden Pheasant tippet*
Body: *Flat silver tinsel or Lurex*
Rib: *Oval silver tinsel*
Hackle: *Grass-green cock hackle*
Wing: *Barred Teal flank*
Head: *Black*

1

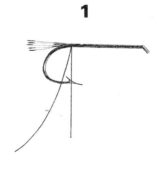

Take the thread down the hook to the bend and tie in a small bunch of Golden Pheasant tippet fibres for the tail. Tie in some oval silver tinsel at the same place.

2

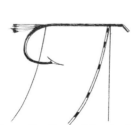

Return the thread back along the shank to the eye and tie in a length of flat silver tinsel or Lurex.

3

Take the flat silver tinsel or Lurex down the shank and back again to form the body, and follow this with the oval silver tinsel. Trim off the excess tinsel. Tie in a bunch of green cock-hackle fibres under the hook to form a false or beard hackle.

4

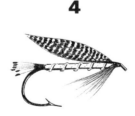

Tie in the wing. See note on soft feather wing materials (page 78).

White Moth

This is a traditional wet-fly pattern to imitate a wide number of light-coloured moths. I have found this fly very effective at dusk on rough streams. (The body of the pattern depicted in the photograph is grey – other versions have an all-white body).

Hook: *Down-eyed 8-14*
Thread: *Pre-waxed white or grey*
Tail: *White cock-hackle fibres*
Body: *Pale-grey fur or wool*
Rib: *Fine silver wire*
Hackle: *White cock-hackle fibres*
Wing: *White Duck wing quill*
Head: *White*

1

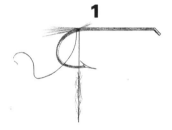

Take the thread down the shank to the bend and tie in a bunch of the white cock-hackle fibres for the tail. Also tie in the fine silver wire for the rib. Dub the pale-grey fur or wool onto the thread.

2

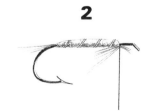

Take the dubbed thread back up the shank to form the body. Follow this with the rib. Underneath the hook tie in a bunch of white cock-hackle fibres.

3

Select a slip of white Duck wing quill from a right feather and the same from a left feather and tie in on top of the hook. Finish the fly in the usual way.

4

This is the all-white version with the wings set more upright. It is also tail-less.

Woodcock & Hare's Ear

This fly is a variation of the well-loved Gold-ribbed Hare's Ear. It is usually used on rivers, but I have known it used on still waters with some degree of success. Its natural coloration no doubt imitates a wide variety of aquatic flies.

Hook: *Down-eyed 10-14*
Thread: *Pre-waxed dark olive*
Tip: *Flat gold tinsel*
Tail: *Bronze Mallard*
Body: *Hare's ear*
Rib *(optional)*: *Fine gold wire*
Wing: *Woodcock wing*
Head: *Olive*

1

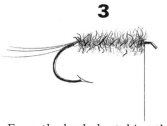

Take the thread down the hook to the bend and tie in a length of the flat gold tinsel.

2

Take a couple of turns of the tinsel around the hook to form the tip. Secure and cut away the tinsel. Now tie in a few fibres of bronze Mallard for the tail, and at the same place tie in a length of the fine gold wire for the rib, if you are going to use one. Dub the hare's ear onto the thread.

3

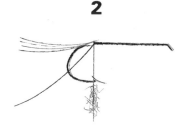

Form the body by taking the fur-laden thread up the shank. Rib with the fine gold wire. The body is now complete.

4

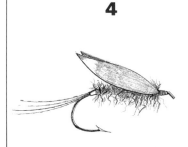

Place two slips of Woodcock wing feather back-to-back and tie in on top of the hook. Finish off the fly in the usual way, and pick out some of the body fur to act as legs or hackle.

IV
Lures &
Streamers

Banded Squirrel Bucktail

A simple bucktail pattern devised by Taff Price and first published in his book *Lures for Game, Coarse, and Sea Fishing* in the early 1970s. This fairly sombre fly, with just a touch of colour in its make-up, proved highly successful for brown trout, although rainbows are not averse to taking it, either.

Hook: *Down-eyed 6-10 long shank*
Thread: *Black*
Tail: *Mixed red and white cock-hackle fibres*
Body: *Mauve wool*
Rib: *Fine oval silver tinsel*
Hackle: *Red and white cock-hackle fibres mixed together*
Wing: *Grey squirrel hair*
Head: *Black*

1

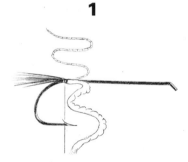

Take the thread down the hook and tie in the tail fibres of mixed red and white cock. At the same place tie in the fine oval silver tinsel for the rib and a length of mauve wool. Return the thread back up the shank.

2

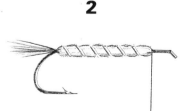

Wind on the wool to form the body and follow this with the rib.

3

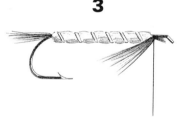

Underneath the throat, tie in a bunch of mixed red and white hackle fibres.

4

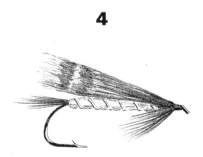

Take a small bunch of grey squirrel hair and tie in on top of the hook. Hairwings/bucktail wings will last longer if, at this stage, some quick-drying adhesive is applied to the wing roots. Form a neat head, whip finish, varnish, and the fly is complete.

Black Bear Hair

This fly was invented by Cliff Henry, who fished for many years at Bough Beech reservoir in Kent in England. It is tied in the New Zealand style. The bear hair must project out of the back so that it is activated on the retrieve. A similar fly can be tied using long-haired black rabbit fur.

Hook: *Down-eyed 8-12 long shank*
Thread: *Black*
Body: *Black seal's fur or substitute*
Rib: *Oval silver tinsel*
Wing: *Black bear hair*
Head: *Black*

1

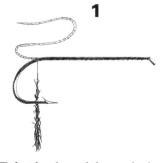

Take the thread down the hook to the bend and there tie in a length of the oval silver tinsel. Dub the black seal's fur onto the thread.

2

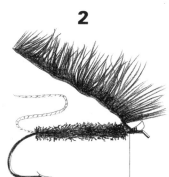

Take the fur-laden thread up the body and tie in a strip of the black bear hair. This should project just beyond the hook.

3

Secure the bear hair at the bend of the hook by means of the oval silver tinsel, and continue the tinsel up the body to the head to form the rib. Tie off, cut away any surplus tinsel, form a neat head, and finish the fly in the normal way.

Black Muddler

This fly, an adaption of the famous Muddler Minnow, was originated by the late Richard Walker. In all of Walker's muddler patterns he dispensed with the flanking oak Turkey wing. Of all the muddler patterns this one is my favourite.

Hook: *Down-eyed 8-10 long shank*
Thread: *Black*
Body: *Black floss silk*
Rib: *Fine oval silver tinsel*
Wing: *Black squirrel tail hair*
Head: *Deer hair*

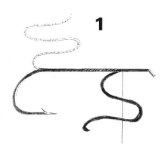

1

Start the thread a third of the way down the shank, then take the thread on down the shank to the bend. At this point tie in a length of fine oval silver tinsel for the rib. Return the thread back up the shank to the starting point and tie in a length of black floss silk.

2

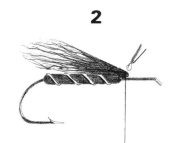

Take the floss silk down the shank and back again to form the body. Follow this with the rib. Remove any surplus silk and tinsel after tying off. Select a bunch of black squirrel tail hair and tie in on top of the hook. Varnish the roots of the hair and allow to dry.

3

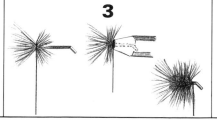

Cut off a small bunch of deer hair and lay on top of the hook. Tie this in by means of three turns of the "soft loop" method. On the third turn pull the thread downwards. This causes the hair to spin around the hook. Using the empty case of a ball-point pen, tamp the hair in tight. Repeat the procedure until the head is complete.

4

Whip finish and varnish the head. Now trim the deer hair to shape with a pair of scissors. A flame from a match, taper, or lighter can smooth out any unwanted stray fibres.

Breathalizer

This pattern was created in the late 1960s by Alec Iles for fishing Chew Valley. It is especially for those times when the trout feed on fry. He adapted some North American patterns to produce this streamer. The pattern first appeared in John Veniard's book *Lake and Reservoir Flies*, 1970.

Hook: *Down-eyed 6-10 long shank*
Thread: *Black*
Tail: *Soft black cock- or hen-hackle fibres*
Body: *Flat silver tinsel*
Rib (optional): *Fine silver wire*
Hackle: *Collar badger hackle (white or cream with a black centre)*
Wing: *Two hot-orange hackles back-to-back with two Green Highlander hackles on the outside*
Cheek: *Jungle Cock*
Head: *Black*

This fly is tied in the same way as the Painted Lady (page 122).

Cat's Whisker

This pattern was invented by David Train. The name comes from the fact that he included a couple of cat's whiskers in the wing (to help control it). My own cat has perfect whiskers for this fly but is somewhat reluctant to give them up, so I generally tie the pattern up without. It does not seem to affect the performance of the fly, which, sadly, makes a bit of a nonsense out of the name.

Hook: *Up-eyed 6-8 long shank*
Thread: *Pre-waxed white or black*
Tail: *White Marabou*
Rib: *Oval gold or silver tinsel*
Body: *Fluorescent yellow chenille*
Wing: *White Marabou (incorporating the white cat's whiskers)*
Eyes: *Metallic bead chain*
Head: *Black*

1

Take the thread down the shank to the bend and there tie in a bunch of white Marabou. At the same place tie in the ribbing tinsel and a length of fluorescent yellow chenille.

2

Take the thread back along the shank and follow this with first the chenille and then the ribbing tinsel. Tie off and cut away any surplus chenille and tinsel. Tie in the wing of white Marabou on top of the hook.

3

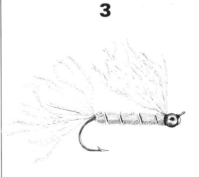

Tie in a pair of bead chain eyes. I always secure these after tying with a drop of super-glue in order to prevent them from revolving around the shank. You will note that in the pattern photographed the eyes are tied beneath the hook. They can if you wish be tied on top. The fly will then swim upside down, which can be an advantage when you are fishing close to the bottom.

Chief Needahbeh

This streamer appears in many British books on flytying because it was one of the few streamer patterns published by John Veniard in his classic *Fly Dresser's Guide*. The fly is named after its creator, Chief Needahbeh of the Penobscot Indians of Maine in the United States. It is a good all-rounder, used for both trout and as a trolling fly for land-locked salmon. Some also use it for black bass.

Hook: *Down-eyed 6-10 long shank*
Thread: *Black*
Tail: *None (although it is sometimes dressed with a slip of red Duck or Goose)*
Tag: *Oval silver tinsel*
Body: *Red floss silk*
Rib: *Flat silver tinsel*
Hackle: *Two: red and yellow mixed and tied as a collar (see note)*
Wing: *Four dyed cock hackles, two red with two yellow on the outside*
Cheek: *Jungle Cock*
Head: *Black*

The fly is tied in the same way as the Painted Lady (page 122), except for the hackle, which is tied as a collar after the wing has been put on (see the drawings). Two hackles are tied in and wound through each other. The use of yellow and red gives an overall orange appearance to the fly.

Christmas Tree

This is a British pattern. Another pattern of the same name is used for steelhead and other game fish on the rivers of the American West right up into Alaska. This fly, however, was devised as an attractor lure for the large man-made lake known as Rutland Water. It was first tied by Alan Dun and seen by Les Lewis while they were fishing at Rutland. This is Lewis's pattern.

Hook: *Down-eyed 6-10 long shank*
Thread: *Black*
Tail: *Fluorescent magenta wool*
Body: *Black chenille*
Rib: *Oval gold tinsel*
Hackle (optional): *Black cock*
Wing: *Black Marabou*
Cheek: *Fluorescent lime-green wool*
Head: *Black*

1

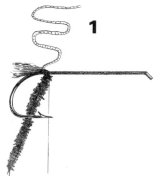

Take the thread down to the hook and tie in the magenta wool tail. At the same point tie in a length of black chenille and a piece of oval gold tinsel.

2

Return the thread up the shank and follow this with the black chenille. Wind on the oval gold tinsel in even turns, tie off, and cut away any surplus chenille or tinsel.

3

If you want a hackle, tie in a bunch of black cock-hackle fibres. Tie in a bunch of Marabou for the wing.

4

Tie two pieces of lime-green fluorescent wool on either side of the wing. Finish the fly in the usual manner.

Concorde

This fly, with its ultra-long nose, is aptly named after the famous supersonic airliner. It was devised by Bob Church and Peter Gathercole. Its design owes a lot to the type of flies used by the saltwater angler when fishing for tarpon and other sea game fish. This pattern stood me in good stead recently when I was fishing for bonefish in Los Roques, Venezuela. Bob Church recommends it for some of Britain's larger reservoirs.

Hook: *Down-eyed 6-10 long shank*
Thread: *Pre-waxed black*
Tail: *Grizzle hackles and red skunk hair (or dyed bucktail)*
Hackle: *Grizzle hackle dyed red*
Body: *Bronze Candlelight or Goldfingering*
Head: *Black*

1

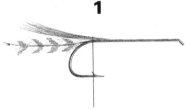

Take the thread down the shank to the bend and there tie in a couple of grizzle hackles and a bunch of red skunk hair over for the tail.

2

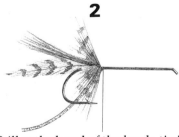

Still at the bend of the hook, tie in two dyed-red grizzle hackles and wind on. Tie off and cut away any surplus feather. Now tie in a length of bronze Candlelight or Goldfingering in front of the hackle.

3

Return the thread down the shank and follow this with the candlelight. Finish the fly in the usual manner.

Goldfingering and Candlelight
These materials are usually found in shops that sell knitting wool. They are man-made fibres interlaced with a non-tarnish tinsel and are used mainly for combining with knitting wool to give a little flash and glitter to the finished garment. Such shops can often provide the flytier with a wealth of tinsels, wools, and unusual yarns.

Don's Perch Fry

This fly was created in the 1970s by the present President of the Fly Dresser's Guild (Great Britain), Donald Downes, who has collaborated with John Veniard on many books. The fly is worth using on waters that have a resident population of perch, as trout feed upon the fry of these bait fish from July onwards. This pattern was first given by John Veniard in *Lake and Reservoir Flies*.

Hook: *Down-eyed 6-8 long shank*
Thread: *Pre-waxed black or olive*
Tail: *White cock-hackle fibres*
Body: *Clear polythene (this can be wound over an underbody of flat silver tinsel or Lurex)*
Wing: *Two brown cock hackles marked with a black marker pen (a well-marked grizzle hackle dyed brown can also be used)*
Hackle: *Scarlet cock-hackle fibres*
Head: *Black*

2

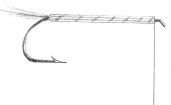

Return the thread back up the shank and then wrap the polythene around the shank to form the body. Do this carefully, as narrow strips of polythene tend to snap fairly easily. A little practice soon tells you how much tension you can apply to the wrappings.

4

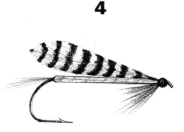

On top of the hook tie in the two barred cock hackles for the wing. Finish the fly in the normal way.

1

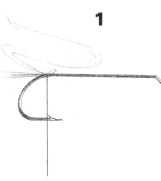

Take the thread down the hook to the bend and tie in the tail fibres. At the same point tie in a length of clear polythene.

3

Underneath the hook, tie in a few scarlet cock-hackles fibres in a beard hackle.

Edson Dark Tiger

This is one of the classic bucktail patterns from the eastern United States. It was created in 1929 by William R. Edson of Portland, Maine. He also created the sister pattern, the Edson Light Tiger.

Hook: *Down-eyed 8-10 long shank*
Thread: *Pre-waxed black*
Tail: *Barred Wood Duck flank*
Body: *Yellow chenille*
Hackle: *Scarlet cock-hackle fibres*
Wing: *Brown bucktail*
Cheek: *Jungle Cock*
Head: *Black*

Sometimes the originator gave his flies a cheek of shaped gold tinsel rather than one of Jungle Cock.

1

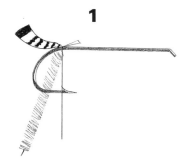

Take the thread down the shank to the bend and tie in a strip of barred Wood Duck flank for the tail. At the same place, tie in a length of yellow chenille.

2

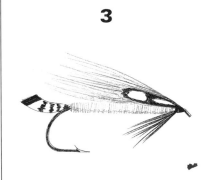

Return the thread back along the shank and follow with the yellow chenille. Secure the chenille and cut off any surplus. Tie in a bunch of scarlet cock-hackle fibres beneath the hook.

3

Tie in the bucktail wing and flank with the Jungle Cock cheeks. Finish the fly in the usual way.

Floating Fry

Reservoir trout feed on a wide range of creatures. At certain times, usually late summer, they become pisciverous, for the water is generally abundant with the fry of many species of fish. The trout usually rampage into such shoals, killing and stunning the small fish, then retreating a little way off before returning to mop up the dead and wounded fish usually found at the surface. The Floating Fry is tied to represent such dead or wounded minnows.

Hook: *Down-eyed 6-12 long shank*
Thread: *Pre-waxed black*
Tail and Back: *White Ethafoam or similar foam plastic*
Body: *Mylar or other plastic tubing*
Hackle: *Scarlet cock*
Head: *Black*

1

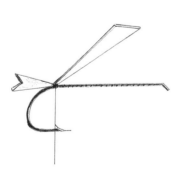

Cut a strip of foam about 5mm (¼") wide and long enough to fit the size of hook. Take the thread down the shank to the bend and there tie in the foam. Cut a notch in the tail part of the foam. Tie in a length of the thread, which will be used to secure the body tubing. Return the thread down the shank and make a couple of half hitches, then cut this piece of tying thread off.

2

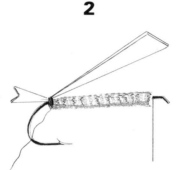

Remove any centre core from the plastic tubing and slip the tubing onto the hook. Secure the tubing with the thread left for this purpose and finish with a couple of half hitches. Wind another piece of tying thread onto the hook.

3

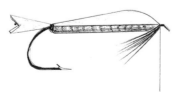

Tie off the tubing at the eye end, bring the plastic foam over the back, and tie off. Tie in a bunch of scarlet cock hackles beneath the hook.

4

Finish the fly with a whip finish and varnish. When the varnish is dry, paint on a white eye with a black pupil.

Golden Shiner

This bucktail lure was devised by Keith Fulsher of Eastchester, New York and is one of a series called the Thunder Creek Series. All these flies are proven fish takers. Others in the series are the Black-nosed Dace, Little Brown Trout, Silver Shiner, and Redfin shiner. All are tied in the same style.

Hook: *Down-eyed 6-10 long shank*
Thread: *Red*
Body: *Flat gold tinsel*
Back: *Brown bucktail*
Stripe: *Yellow bucktail*
Underbody: *White bucktail*
Head: *Formed by the reversed bucktail*
Eye: *Yellow with black pupil*

1

Wind the thread a little way down the shank as shown and tie in a bunch of white bucktail under the hook. At the same point, but on top of the hook, tie in a bunch of yellow bucktail with a bunch of brown bucktail over this. The bunches must be quite sparse and all of them must project beyond the eye.

2

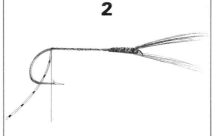

Take the thread the rest of the way down the shank to the bend and tie in the flat gold tinsel for the body.

3

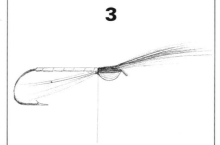

Return the thread back along the shank and follow with the tinsel. Tie off and cut away the surplus tinsel. Now take the thread right up to the eye, covering the hair above and below the hook. Move the thread back a little to allow space for the head. Reverse the white under-hair first and tie off. The underbody is now formed and so is the under portion of the head.

4

Now bring the yellow hair over the back and secure. Follow this with the brown bucktail. Tie off. The red thread simulates the gills of the small fish. Finish the fly behind the head and coat the turns of thread and the head with clear varnish.

5

When the varnish is dry, paint on a yellow eye with a black pupil.

GOLDIE

Goldie

This lure, credited to Bob Church, was devised in the late 1970s for reservoir fishing. It is normally fished deep, but I have taken fish with it at all depths. It is a good lure for cloudy, muddy water.

Hook: *Down-eyed 6-12 long shank*
Thread: *Black*
Tail: *Yellow cock-hackle fibres*
Body: *Flat gold tinsel*
Rib: *Fine gold wire*
Hackle: *Yellow cock hackle*
Wing: *Yellow goat hair or dyed squirrel, with black hair over*
Head: *Black*

This fly is tied in the same way as the Banded Squirrel Bucktail (page 101), except for the wing, which in this case consists of two bunches of hair, one on top of the other, the black forming a roof to the yellow (see the drawing).

Gray Ghost

One of the best-known American patterns, this was devised by the famous Carrie Stevens in 1924. The pattern must not be confused with the New Zealand fly of the same name. The red band on the head of the fly was Carrie Stevens' trademark. She incorporated this foible into all her streamer patterns.

Hook: *Down-eyed 6-8 long shank*
Thread: *Pre-waxed black*
Tip: *Flat silver tinsel*
Body: *Orange floss silk*
Rib: *Flat silver tinsel*
Underwing or throat: *Peacock herl, white bucktail, and Golden Pheasant crest*
Wing: *Golden Pheasant crest and grey cock hackles*
Shoulder: *Silver Pheasant hackle*
Cheek: *Jungle Cock or substitute*
Head: *Black with a red band (the band is optional)*

1

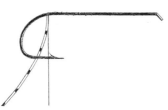

Take the thread down the shank to the bend and tie in a length of the flat silver tinsel.

2

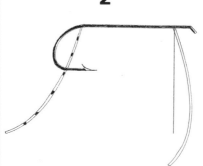

Return the thread back along the shank and tie in a length of orange floss silk.

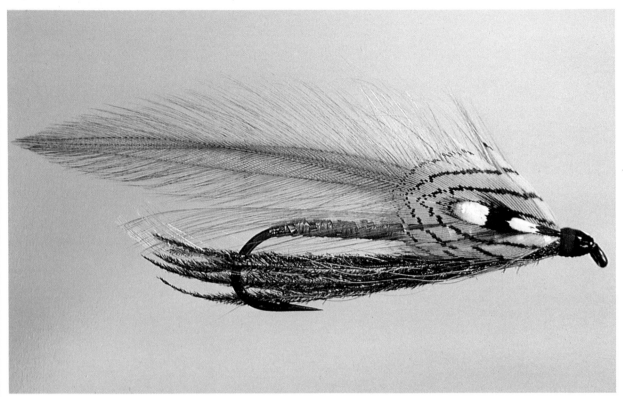

GRAY GHOST

3

Wind the floss silk down the shank and back again to form the body, tie off, and cut away the surplus silk. Take a few turns of the flat silver tinsel around the bend of the hook to form the tip and then take the tinsel up the shank to form the rib. Tie off.

4

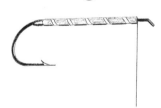

Under the hook tie in a few fibres of the white bucktail and four strands of the Peacock herl.

5

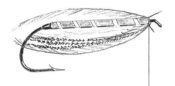

Tie in one Golden Pheasant crest under the hook, pointing upwards, and another on top of the hook, pointing downwards.

6

Select four grey cock hackles of the same size and place them back-to-back and tie on top of the hook.

7

Take two Silver Pheasant hackles and strip off the soft flue. Then take two Jungle Cock feathers and coat their underside with a dab of quick-setting adhesive and place them on the Silver Pheasant feathers.

8

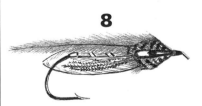

Tie these two glued feathers on either side of the wing. Complete the fly in the usual manner and add a circle of red if you wish to emulate Carrie Stevens.

Green Sweeny

The famous Sweeny Todd fly created by Richard Walker remains one of the most popular lures in the armoury of the still-water angler. This variant can be very effective. On the original fly the fluorescent collar was magenta, while in this version it is, as the name suggests, green.

Hook: *Down-eyed 6-10 long shank*
Thread: *Pre-waxed black*
Tail: *None*
Body: *Black floss silk*
Rib: *Oval silver tinsel*
Thorax/Collar: *Fluorescent green floss silk*
Hackle (optional): *Black cock*
Wing: *Dyed black squirrel tail*
Head: *Black*

1

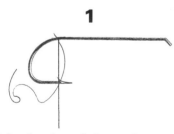

Take the thread down the shank to the bend and tie in a length of the oval silver tinsel.

2

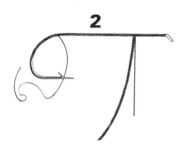

Return the thread up the shank and tie in a length of the black floss silk.

3

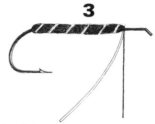

Wind the silk down the body and back again, tie off, and cut away any surplus. Wind the oval silver tinsel up the body, tie off, and cut away surplus. Tie in a length of fluorescent green floss silk.

4

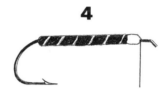

Wind on the fluorescent green silk as a collar, tie off, and cut away any surplus.

5

Tie in a bunch of black squirrel tail on top of the hook. A dab of quick-setting adhesive at the roots helps secure the hair. Finish off the fly with a neat head, whip finish, and varnish.

Grizzly King

This lure is an adaptation of a traditional American trout fly. It is used for most species of game fish, including both the Pacific and Atlantic salmon, as well as for trout. The fly is credited to Gardner Percy of Maine.

Hook: *Up-eyed 6-10 long shank*
Thread: *Pre-waxed black*
Tip: *Flat gold tinsel*
Tail: *Scarlet cock-hackle fibres*
Body: *Green floss floss*
Rib: *Flat gold tinsel*
Wing: *Grey squirrel tail*
Hackle: *Grizzle cock tied as a collar*
Head: *Black*

Follow the instructions for the Polar Shrimp (page 137) and substitute the appropriate materials.

Hamill's Killer

Another pattern from New Zealand and, like Mrs Simpson, it is tied in the "Killer" style with the wing feathers flanking the hook. It was first tied by Bill Hamill of Roturua and was supposed to imitate the small indigenous bait fish, Cock-a-Bully, which is similar to the British Miller's Thumb or Bullhead and the American Bullhead Minnow. The pattern can be either red- or yellow-bodied. The red is generally used during the night and the yellow during the day. More up-to-date versions sometimes use a green body.

Hook: *Down-eyed 1-10 long shank*
Thread: *Pre-waxed black*
Tail: *Black squirrel tail*
Body: *Wool: red, green, or yellow*
Wing: *Grey Partridge dyed green*
Head: *Black*

This fly is tied in exactly the same way as the more famous Mrs Simpson (page 119). Follow the instructions for this pattern and substitute with the appropriate materials.

Leprechaun

This fly goes back to the early 1970s and was devised by Peter Wood. I have found it to be a useful pattern towards the end of the season, while others maintain that it is best during a bloom of green algae or, as sometimes occurs on reservoirs, a population explosion of green Daphnia. This fly is now more often than not tied Matuka-style.

Hook: *Down-eyed 8-10 long shank*
Thread: *Black*
Tail: *Bright-green cock-hackle fibres*
Body: *Fluorescent lime-green chenille*
Rib: *Flat silver tinsel*
Hackle: *Bright-green cock hackle*
Wing: *Four bright-green cock hackles*
Head: *Black*

The dressing of this pattern poses no great problems. It is tied in the same way as the Painted Lady (page 122). This pattern uses chenille instead of floss for the body. It is tied in at the tail end and wound up the shank to form the body. The chenille has a centre core which should be exposed and the chenille attached to the hook by this (see the drawings).

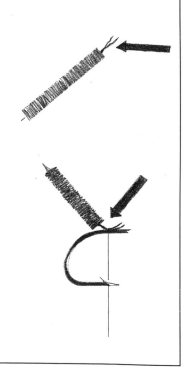

115

Mini Muddler Soldier Palmer

This lure is one of a series of patterns that combine the muddler-minnow concept with the traditional lake wet fly. It is used generally as a top dropper on a team of wet flies while fishing "on the top" in the traditional loch style. The clipped deer hair head adds extra buoyancy to the fly.

Hook: *Down-eyed 10-12 short shank*
Thread: *Brown*
Tail: *Red wool*
Body: *Red wool (or a dubbing of red fur)*
Rib: *Fine oval gold tinsel*
Hackle: *Palmered natural light-red cock*
Head: *Clipped deer hair*

1

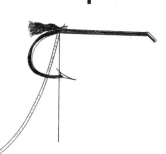

After taking the thread down the shank to the bend, tie in a tuft of red wool for the tail and a length of fine oval gold tinsel for the rib.

2

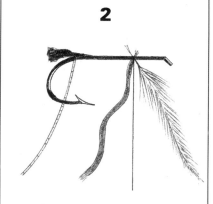

Return the thread two-thirds of the way up the shank and tie in a length of the red wool and a natural light-red cock hackle by the stalk. If a dubbed body is required, the fur should be dubbed onto the thread before winding it back along the shank.

3

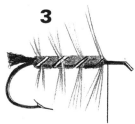

Take the red wool down the shank and back again to form the body. Wind the hackle down the shank and secure this with the first turn of the fine oval gold tinsel. Then take the tinsel carefully along the body, securing the hackle as you go along. Any trapped fibres can be eased out with a dubbing needle after this has been done. Trim off the hackle point and cut off any surplus tinsel.

4

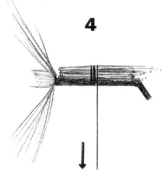

Take a small bunch of natural deer-body hair and place on top of the shank. Take three turns of thread around the hair and pull down tight after the third turn, to make the hair flair out around the shank.

5

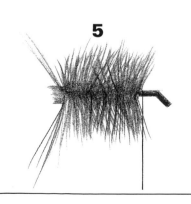

Continue to spin the deer hair until the shank is filled up.

6

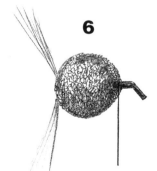

Trim the deer hair to a ball-like shape.

7

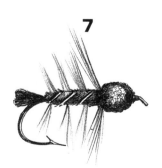

Finish off the fly in the usual way.

Minnow Streamer

Another Taff Price pattern, this is a more imitative fly than the Painted Lady. This time the lure is created to imitate a small minnow bait fish. It should be fished much as the natural fish would behave, quite slowly at times but interspersed with a faster retrieve.

Hook: *Down-eyed 6-10 long shank*
Thread: *Olive*
Tail: *Blue-dun cock-hackle fibres*
Body: *White floss silk*
Rib: *Oval silver tinsel*
Hackle: *Red (scarlet) cock-hackle fibres at the throat*
Wing: *Olive cock hackles*
Cheek: *Barred Teal feathers on either side of the wing*
Head: *Olive; varnish on the top, white beneath*

This pattern is tied streamer-style in the same way as the Painted Lady (page 122).

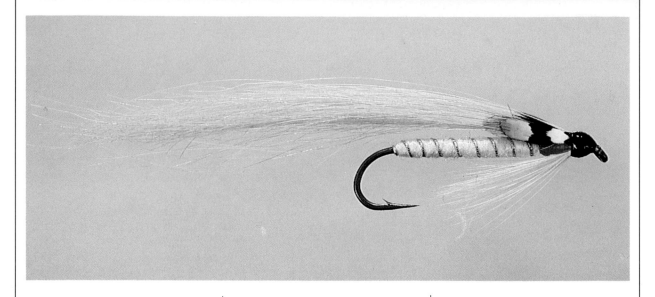

Mrs Palmer

This lure with the extra-long wing was created by the late Richard Walker. I have found it to be very effective when the water is murky.

Hook: *Down-eyed 6-10 long shank*
Thread: *Pre-waxed black*
Body: *Fluorescent white wool with a fluorescent orange portion under the hackle*
Rib: *Fine oval silver tinsel*
Hackle: *White cock-hackle fibres*
Wing: *Pale-yellow goat hair, twice the length of the shank*
Cheek: *Jungle Cock or substitute*
Head: *Black*

1

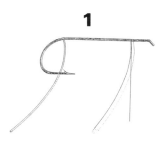

First take the thread down the shank to the bend and there tie in a length of fine oval silver tinsel for the rib. Return the thread back along the shank to the point

shown and there tie in a length of fluorescent white wool.

2

Form the body by winding the wool down the shank and back again (if the wool is a little thick you can tie it in at the tail end with the ribbing tinsel and only wind it once up the shank). Follow the wool body with the ribbing tinsel in even turns. Secure and cut off any surplus material. At this point tie in a length of fluorescent orange wool.

3

Wind on the orange wool and secure.

4

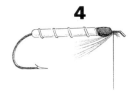

Tie in a bunch of white cock-hackle fibres under the hook.

5

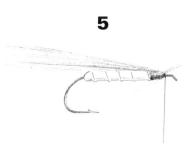

Take a bunch of pale-yellow goat hair, twice the length of the hook shank, and tie in on top of the hook.

6

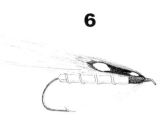

Flank the wing with two Jungle Cock feathers. Finish the fly with a neat head, whip finish, and varnish.

Mrs Simpson

This New Zealand pattern is widely used in Australia, Southern Africa, and Britain as well as in its country of origin. It is tied in the "Killer" style, with the wing feathers flanking the hook.

Hook: *Down-eyed 6-10 long shank*
Thread: *Pre-waxed black*
Tail: *Black squirrel hair*
Body: *Red or yellow wool*
Wing: *Cock Pheasant rump feathers*
Head: *Black*

1

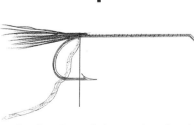

Take the thread down the shank to the bend and there tie in a bunch of black squirrel hair for the tail. At the same point tie in a length of wool (yellow or red depending on the pattern required).

2

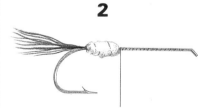

Return the thread a little way up the shank to the point shown and follow this with the wool. Secure the wool.

3

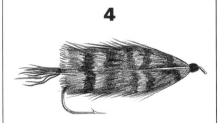

Tie in on either side of the hook two cock Pheasant rump feathers. Repeat this wool and feather application three times. The feathers should overlap each other so that the finished fly looks as though it was flanked with just two feathers and not with the three pairs.

4

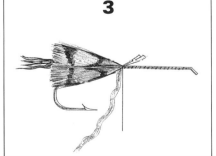

Complete the fly with a neat head, whip finish, and varnish.

Nailer

This pattern comes into its own as the weather and, of course, the water warms up. Trout then seem to favour a more soberly dressed lure, and the Nailer fits this category. Some prefer to tie this fly up as a hairwing, but both styles have their adherents.

Hook: *Down-eyed 6-10 long shank*
Thread: *Black*
Tail: *Scarlet cock-hackle fibres*
Body: *Flat gold tinsel*
Rib: *Fine gold wire*
Hackle: *Four turns of long-fibred brown cock*
Wing: *Four scarlet dyed cock hackles with two strips of oak Turkey flanking*
Head: *Black*

Again, this is a pretty basic streamer pattern tied in the same way as the Painted Lady (page 122). Follow the instructions for this fly, substituting the appropriate materials. Instead of the Jungle Cock cheek used in the Painted Lady, this pattern has two strips of oak Turkey taken from a left and right feather. These should be tied in so that they roof the cock hackles, as shown. For the hairwing version, red goat or skunk is roofed by brown goat or skunk. The rest of the fly is the same as above.

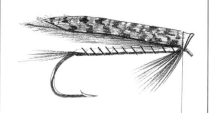

Ombudsman

This fly was created by Brian Clarke and given in his excellent book, *The Pursuit of Stillwater Trout.* It imitates a number of large aquatic nymphs, including the Alder larva. I have heard this fly described as the nymph fisherman's lure, especially when tied as a hair wing.

Hook: *Down-eyed 8-10 long shank*
Thread: *Pre-waxed brown*
Body: *Bronze Peacock herl*
Rib: *Copper wire*
Wing: *Mottled brown hen or Turkey*
Hackle: *A long soft, brown cock hackle*
Head: *Brown*

The head of the fly is tied in an elongated fashion.

1

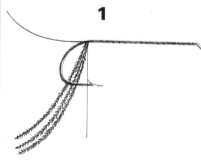

Take the thread down the hook to the bend and tie in a length of the copper wire and three or four strands of bronze Peacock herl.

2

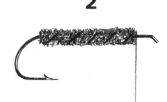

Form a rope with the thread and the herl and wind it up the shank to form the body. Follow this with the copper wire. You can in fact form a rope with the copper wire, thread, and herl and wind it all together back up the shank to the point shown (ensure that you have room for a long head to the fly). Cut away any surplus herl and wire after tying off.

3

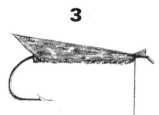

Select two matching slips of wing feather from a right and left wing quill and tie in on either side of the hook, half flanking the body.

4

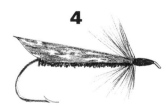

Finish off the fly with a long, soft, brown cock hackle. Whip finish an elongated head and varnish.

Painted Lady

This is a pattern created by Taff Price in the early 1970s as an attractor lure. He had been tying some built-wing salmon flies and, not wishing to waste the bits and pieces left on his bench, he produced the Painted Lady from the leftovers. It is used as a general black lure and must not be confused with the steelhead pattern of the same name from the western United States.

Hook: *Down-eyed 6-8 long shank*
Thread: *Black*
Tail: *Guinea Fowl dyed blue*
Body: *Black floss silk*
Rib: *Oval silver tinsel*
Hackle: *Magenta cock hackle*
Wing: *Black cock hackles*
Cheek (optional): *Jungle Cock or substitute*
Head: *Black*

1

Take the thread down the hook to the bend and tie in some dyed-blue Guinea Fowl. At the same place tie in a length of the oval silver tinsel. Return the thread back up the shank to the point shown and tie in a length of black floss silk.

2

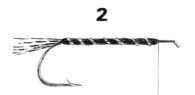

Take the black floss silk down the body and back again, tie off, and cut off any surplus. Follow this with even turns of the oval silver tinsel for the rib.

3

Wind in the magenta cock hackle.

4

Select four identical black cock hackles and remove any of the soft flue around the base of the stalks. Now place them together, dull sides in, offer them to the top of the hook so that they point over the eye, and take a few turns over the stalks to secure.

Holding the hackles in the thumb and finger, pull them up and over so that they now point towards the bend of the hook.

5

Wrap the loop made by the stalks with the tying thread (see detail). This form of winging makes it difficult to pull the finished wings out.

6

If you want cheeks, select two Jungle Cock feathers and flank the wing with them. Form a neat head, whip finish, and then varnish.

Poodle

This highly mobile black Marabou lure was devised by John Wadham for fishing Rutland Water. I suppose one could describe this lure as a cross between a "Matuka" and an "Aztec", using Marabou instead of the usual feather or wool. Sometimes dyed black Arctic Fox is used for a more durable fly.

POODLE

Hook: *Down-eyed 6-10 long shank*
Thread: *Pre-waxed black*
Tail: *Black Marabou*
Body: *Black chenille*
Wing: *Three or four bunches of black Marabou, depending on the size of hook used*
Head: *Black*

1

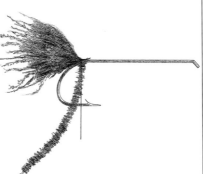

Take the thread down the shank to the bend and tie in a generous bunch of black Marabou for the tail. At the same point tie in a length of black chenille.

2

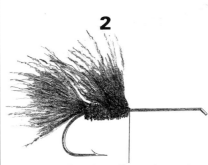

Wind on the chenille to the point shown, where you tie in another bunch of black Marabou.

3

Repeat this procedure until the hook is full, leaving a turn of chenille free at the head.

Red Setter

This fly originated in New Zealand, where it was created by G. Sanderson of Turangi. It is tied in the "Fuzzy Wuzzy" style, with the hackle halfway down the body. The Red Setter is a popular fly in Australia and Southern Africa as well as in its native country. It is recommended as a dusk fly and should be fished quite deep.

Hook: *Down-eyed 8-10 long shank*
Thread: *Brown*
Tail: *Brown squirrel-tail fibres*
Body: *Orange chenille*
Hackle: *Pale-ginger cock*
Head: *Brown*

1

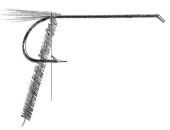

Take the thread down to the bend of the hook and tie in a bunch of brown squirrel-tail fibres. At the same place tie in a length of orange chenille.

2

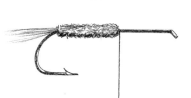

Return the thread halfway up the shank and follow with the chenille body. Cut off any surplus chenille.

3

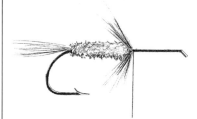

Wind on the pale-ginger cock hackle, and tie in another length of orange chenille. Take the thread towards the eye.

4

Wind on the second half of the chenille body. Then wind on another pale-ginger cock hackle.
Finish the fly in the usual way.

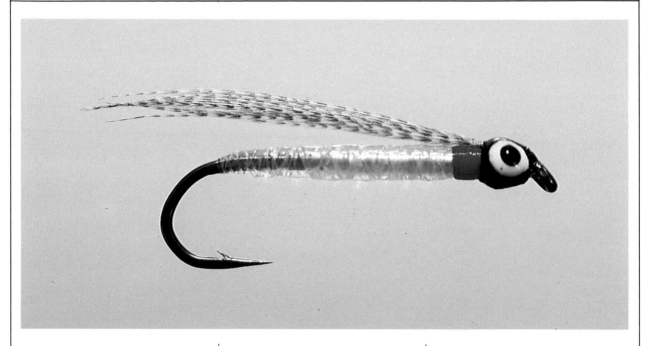

Sinfoil's Fry

This is one of the first translucent-bodied flies to become widespread. Created by Ken Sinfoil, former head bailiff of Weirwood reservoir in Sussex, it resembles a small fry and is a welcome pattern in my fly box for those times when the trout come into the margins to feed upon the shoals of fry.

Hook: *Down-eyed 10 long shank*
Thread: *Black*
Underbody: *Flat silver tinsel (Lurex or Mylar)*
Overbody: *Clear polythene strip*
Collar: *Scarlet floss silk*
Wing: *Barred feather slip, from the poor side of a bronze Mallard, Teal, or Widgeon*
Head: *Black thread with white painted eye*

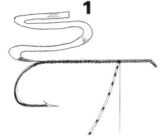

Take the thread down the shank to the bend of the hook and tie in a strip of clear polythene, about 8 mm (5/16") in width. I find 250 gauge polythene to be about right. Return the thread three-quarters of the way back up the shank and tie in a strip of flat silver tinsel. (Lurex or Mylar tinsel are best.)

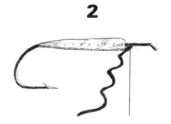

Take the tinsel down the shank and back to form the silver underbody. Tie off and cut away any surplus tinsel. Follow this with tight turns of the polythene strip. Care should be taken lest you break the polythene.

Once the overbody has been formed, tie off and remove any excess polythene.

Wind on a small collar of the scarlet floss silk to imitate the vital organs of the fry.

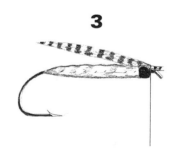

Select a slip of Mallard, Widgeon, or Teal feather, roll it into a wing, and tie in on top of the hook.

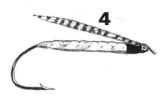

Form a neat head, whip finish, and varnish. When dry, paint on a white eye with a black pupil.

Squirrel & Silver

This is a British reservoir lure devised by John McLellan to imitate coarse-fish fry, on which the large reservoir browns and rainbows feed avidly at the tail end of the season.

Hook: *Down-eyed 8-10 long shank*
Thread: *Pre-waxed black*
Tail: *Fluorescent red wool*
Body: *Flat silver tinsel*
Rib: *Fine oval silver tinsel*
Wing: *Grey squirrel*
Hackle: *Silver Mallard feather fibres tied beneath the hook*
Head: *Black*

Follow the instructions for the Alaska Mary Ann (page 130) and substitute with the materials given above.

Wooly Bugger

This is one of the most consistent fish takers I have known. In the United States it is used on many of the freestone rivers to great effect. In Britain it is used on reservoirs and is even more of a killing pattern. It can be tied up in a variety of different colours, the most effective being black, brown, olive, and white, though I must add that I have found an orange or yellow pattern to be particularly effective in murky water conditions.

Hook: *Down-eyed 4-10 long shank*
Thread: *Pre-waxed black*
Tail: *Marabou feather and Flashabou or similar strips*
Body: *Black wool over lead wire*
Hackle: *Black cock hackle*
Head: *Black*

1

Pre-weight the hook with lead wire and place it in the vice. Take the thread down the shank to the bend and there tie in a generous bunch of Marabou. Tie in two or three strands of Flashabou or similar product on either side of the feather. Now tie in a length of black wool and a large black cock hackle by the tip.

2

Take the thread back up the shank and follow this with the black wool for the body. Finally, palmer the cock hackle along the body and tie off. Complete the fly with the usual whip finish and varnish.

Zonker

This is one of the modern American rabbit-lure patterns. The original rabbit flies came from New Zealand and were tied in the "Matuka" style. This fly was devised by Dan Byford of Colorado and is used for large- and small-mouthed bass as well as for all species of trout.

Hook: *Down-eyed 4-8 long shank*
Thread: *Pre-waxed red or black*
Underbody: *Trimbrite metallic strip or similar product cut to shape*
Body: *Silver Mylar tube*
Wing: *Natural rabbit fur on the skin*
Hackle (optional): *Grizzle cock*
Head: *Red*

There are many colour variations in the Zonker series of flies, such as Black Orange.

1

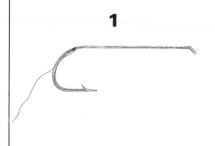

Take a piece of the thread and secure it at the bend of the hook.

2

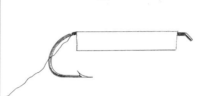

Take a piece of Trimbrite metallic strip and fold it over the shank.

3

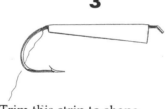

Trim this strip to shape.

4

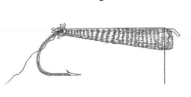

Slip the Mylar tubing over the strip and secure at the bend of the hook with the thread left

there for this purpose. Wind on another length of the tying thread from the eye of the hook.

5

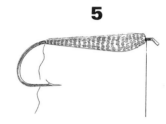

Secure the Mylar at the head end.

6

Cut a strip of about 8 mm (¼") from a rabbit skin and lay it on top of the hook. Tie it down at the bend with the thread left for this purpose. Then tie it down at the head end.

7

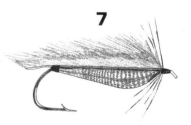

Wind on a grizzle cock hackle and complete the fly in the usual way. Do not forget to coat the turns of thread at the bend with the varnish.

V
STEELHEAD
FLIES

The steelhead trout is a sea-going variation of the rainbow *(Salmo gairdneri)* and is regarded as the Pacific-coast equivalent of the migratory brown trout of Europe. Steelhead are found from California right up to Alaska. They are great travellers and, after their sojourn in the sea, they travel long stretches up their home rivers to spawn. It is not unusual for a steelhead to be caught over 100 miles from the sea.

There are two runs of this sporting trout every year – one in the summer and one in the winter. The winter-run fish are mature fish going upstream to spawn and are usually much bigger than their summer-run counterparts, which have to run in low-water conditions. Many specimens of winter-run steelhead weigh over 20 lbs, and they are usually taken on the deeply fished fly in pools where they rest on their journey. Even though they do not feed in the true sense while migrating, they can be tempted to take a well-presented and attractive-looking fly. As can be imagined, the tackle for these hard-fighting fish has to be well-dimensioned and sturdy, with sinking-line weights of 9 and 10 AFTM weighting being the order of the day. In the low-water conditions that prevail during the summer, the steelhead can often

be tempted to take a fly off the surface.

In the small selection of steelhead-fly patterns given here, there are flies for both winter and summer fishing.

It would appear that the steelhead is especially attracted to orange and white flies, so rather than fill up the pages with flies of these colours we have tried to broaden the scope by including highly effective patterns in other colours. Many of the standard steelhead flies are also effective for sea-run cutthroat trout and some of the Pacific salmon species.

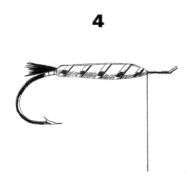

4

Wind the floss or wool down the shank and back again to form the body. Tie off and cut off any surplus. Follow this with the flat silver tinsel for the rib.

Alaska Mary Ann

This classic pattern from Alaska is based on an early Eskimo lure called the Kobuk Hook, a jigging lure fashioned from ivory, polar-bear hair, and a metal nail. This pattern was developed by Frank Dufresne.

Hook: *2-8 salmon hook (can be tied on streamer hooks)*
Thread: *Pre-waxed black*
Tag: *Flat silver tinsel*
Tail: *Red hackle fibres or floss silk*
Body: *Ivory floss or white wool*
Rib: *Flat silver tinsel*
Wing: *White polar bear*
Cheek: *Jungle Cock or substitute*
Head: *Black*

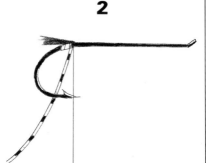

2

Form the tag by wrapping the tinsel around the shank, tie off, and cut off any surplus tinsel. At the same place tie in some red hackle fibres or floss silk, and also another length of the flat silver tinsel.

5

Tie in a bunch of the white polar-bear hair on top of the hook to form the wing. Bind down the root ends.

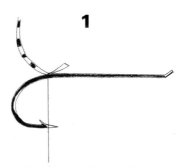

1

Take the thread down the shank to the bend and tie in a strip of the flat silver tinsel.

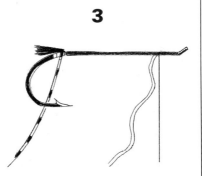

3

Return the thread up the shank and there tie in a length of the ivory floss silk or white wool.

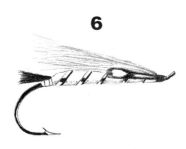

6

Tie in a Jungle Cock feather or substitute on either side of the wing. Finish the fly with a neat head, a whip finish, and varnish.

Babine Special

This is one of the classic "salmon egg" patterns, used for many species of salmon as well as steelhead. It is popular for winter steelhead and is usually fished weighted.

Hook: *2-8 salmon hook*
Thread: *Pre-waxed red or black*
Body: *Fluorescent orange, pink, or red chenille*
Hackle: *Centre hackle: red; front hackle: white*
Head: *Red*

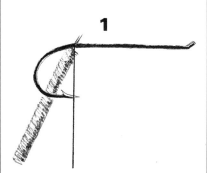

1

(If a weighted fly is required, wrap the shank with lead wire first.) Take the thread down the hook to the bend and tie in a length of the fluorescent chenille you have chosen.

2

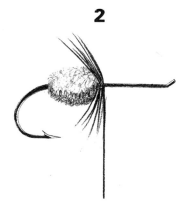

Form a round ball with the chenille, tie off, and remove any excess. Tie in and wind on a red hackle in the middle of the hook.

3

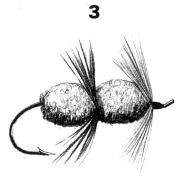

Repeat Step 1 by winding on another ball of chenille and finish with a white hackle at the eye. Complete the fly with a whip finish and varnish.

Boss

There are a number of variations of this fly. The one depicted here is sometimes called the Black Boss. The Orange Boss is in fact the reverse of the Black Boss with an orange chenille body with a black hackle and tail. The pattern is used for both trout and salmon. Similar flies are used on British reservoirs for rainbow trout.

Hook: *2-6 salmon hook*
Thread: *Pre-waxed black*
Tail: *Orange calf tail*
Tag: *Oval or flat silver tinsel*
Body: *Black chenille*
Rib: *Oval or flat silver tinsel*
Hackle: *Hot-orange hackle*
Eyes: *Bead chain*
Head: *Black*

1

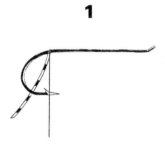

Take the thread down the hook and tie in a length of the silver tinsel for the tag.

2

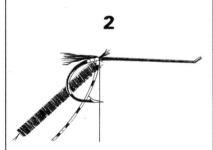

Wind on the tinsel to form the tag, tie off, and remove any excess. At the same place tie in a bunch of the orange calf tail, a length of the black chenille and the ribbing tinsel.

3

Return the thread back up the shank and follow this with the chenille to form the body. Take the ribbing tinsel up the body, tie off, and snip off any surplus.

4

Wind on a hot-orange hackle, collar-style.

5

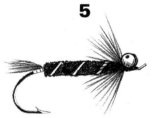

For the eyes, snip off two beads from a bead chain and tie in on top of the hook with a figure-of-eight knot. I always add a dab of instant glue at this stage to prevent the beads revolving around the hook shank. Finish the fly with a whip finish and varnish.

Brad's Brat

This fly was the invention of Enos Bradner of Seattle way back in 1937. It is considered as a classic steelhead fly for most of the Washington rivers.

Hook: *2/0-4 salmon hook*
Thread: *Pre-waxed black*
Tail: *Orange and white bucktail*
Tag: *Silver or gold tinsel*
Body: *Rear half orange wool, front half red wool*
Rib: *Medium silver or gold tinsel*
Wing: *Orange bucktail over white bucktail (calf can also be used).*
Hackle: *Brown cock-hackle fibres*
Head: *Black*

1

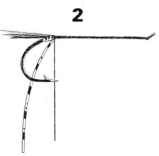

Take the thread down the hook and tie in a length of silver or gold tinsel at the bend.

2

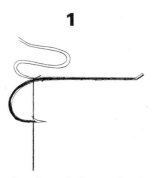

Form a tag with the tinsel and tie off, removing any excess. Now tie in the orange and white bucktail for the tail and at the same point tie in a length of the medium silver or gold ribbing tinsel.

3

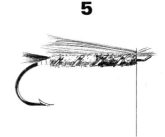

Take the thread half-way up the hook and tie in a length of the orange wool.

4

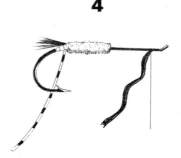

Wind the wool down the shank and back to form half the body. Take the tying thread back to the eye of the hook and tie in a length of the red wool.

5

Complete the body by winding on the red wool. Follow this with the ribbing tinsel. On top of the hook, tie in a bunch of white bucktail or calf tail.

6

On top of the white bucktail tie in a bunch of orange bucktail. Beneath the hook tie in a beard hackle of brown cock. Complete the fly in the usual manner.

Grease Liner

Another summer pattern, used with a floating fly line, this was created by Harry Lemire in 1974. The fly is designed to cause a lot of commotion when it is fished across a fast-moving river current. The head is sometimes soaked in varnish to enhance the action of the fly.

Hook: *4-8 salmon hook light wire*
Thread: *Pre-waxed black*
Tail: *Dark deer hair*
Body: *Black seal's fur or substitute*
Wing: *Dark deer hair*
Head: *Black*

1

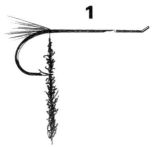

Take the thread down the shank and there tie in a generous bunch of the dark deer hair. Dub the tying thread with some black seal's fur or substitute.

2

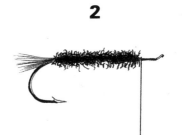

Take the fur-laden thread up the shank to form the body.

3

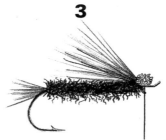

Select another bunch of dark deer hair and tie in on top of the hook to form the wing. Clip the hair ends to form a head on top of the hook only.

4

Finish the fly with a whip finish and varnish.

Kalama Special

This pattern is generally considered to be a fly for summer-run steelheads. The fly was originated by Mike Kennedy of Oswego, Oregon. It is useful as a hopper imitation and is used on such rivers as the Deschutes, and on many salmon rivers. There is a sister pattern called the Kalama Favourite, which has a red body instead of yellow.

Hook: *4-8 salmon hook*
Thread: *Pre-waxed black or yellow*
Tail: *Scarlet cock-hackle fibres*
Body: *Yellow wool*
Hackle: *Badger cock hackle*
Wing: *White bucktail*
Head: *Black*

1

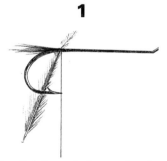

Take the thread down the shank to the bend and tie in a bunch of the scarlet cock-hackle fibres. At the same place tie in a badger cock hackle by the tip.

2

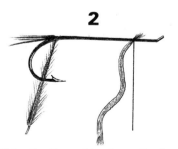

Take the thread back up the hook and tie in a length of the yellow wool.

3

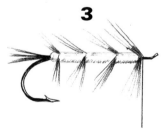

Take the wool down the shank and back to form the body, and wind the badger cock hackle up the body palmer-style. Tie off and cut away surplus feather and wool.

4

Tie in a bunch of white bucktail on top of the hook and finish the fly in the usual way.

A Jungle Cock cheek is sometimes added.

POLAR SHRIMP

Montana Brassy

This very simple fly is used to take most species of salmonoids. It is popular in Alaska.

Hook: *Small sizes of salmon hook*
Thread: *Pre-waxed black*
Body: *Copper wire*
Wing: *White bucktail or calf*
Head: *Black*

2

Return the thread back up the shank and then wind the copper wire in neat coils to form the body. Tie off and remove the surplus wire.

Polar Shrimp

This pattern was devised by Martin Tolley from Canada. It is used throughout the North West of America. Apart from the pattern depicted, there is another version with the body made up of half gold tinsel and half orange chenille.

Hook: *2-8 salmon hook*
Thread: *Pre-waxed red*
Tail: *Red or orange cock-hackle fibres*
Body: *Orange chenille*
Hackle: *Hot-orange cock hackle*
Wing: *White polar bear or calf tail*
Head: *Red*

1

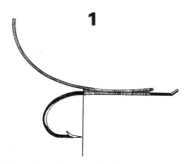

Take the thread half-way down the shank and tie in a length of the copper wire. Bind down the wire with the tying thread.

3

Tie in a bunch of the white bucktail for the wing. Finish the fly with a whip finish and varnish.

1

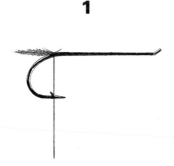

Take the thread down the hook and tie in a bunch of the red or hot-orange cock-hackle fibres.

PURPLE PERIL

Purple Peril

This is one of the patterns used for steelhead that does not have orange, red, yellow, or white in its make-up. Purple can quite often be an attractive colour for many species of game fish, especially steelhead. There are a number of variations of this pattern. One uses a wing of white polar bear, another fox squirrel tail, while the one depicted has a wing of black squirrel or bucktail.

Hook: *2-6 salmon hook (sometimes tied low-water style)*
Thread: *Pre-waxed black*
Tail: *Purple hackle fibres*
Tag: *Flat silver tinsel*
Body: *Purple wool*
Rib: *Flat silver tinsel*
Hackle: *Purple cock hackle*
Wing: *Black hair, fox squirrel, or white polar bear*
Head: *Black*

Follow the instructions for the Polar Shrimp (opposite), with the addition of a tag.

2

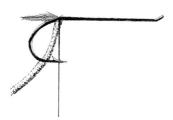

At the same place tie in a length of the orange chenille.

3

Take the thread back up the shank and follow this with the chenille to form the body.

4

Tie in a bunch of white polar-bear hair on top of the hook (calf tail is a good substitute). Trim off the excess hair.

5

Wind on the hot-orange hackle and finish off the fly with a neat head, a whip finish, and varnish.

Russian River Coho

As its name suggests, this pattern was named after the Russian River in Alaska, where it is used for Coho salmon. It is also used to take other species of fish, including steelhead. The fly was devised by Don Holtz of Anchorage.

Hook: *2-6 salmon hook*
Thread: *Pre-waxed black*
Body: *None*
Overwing: *Red bucktail*
Underwing: *White bucktail*
Head: *Black*

1

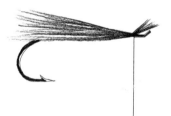

Wind the thread onto the hook at the eye and tie in a bunch of the red bucktail.

2

Reverse the hook in the vice and tie in a bunch of the white bucktail underneath the hook. Finish with a neat head and varnish.

Skagit Coachman

This fly is considered to be a good pattern in murky water conditions. It was devised by Jack De Yonge.

Hook: *2-6 salmon hook*
Thread: *Pre-waxed black*
Tail: *Black bear hair or black hackle*
Body: *In three parts: fluorescent orange chenille, Peacock herl, and fluorescent orange chenille*
Hackle: *Black cock hackle*
Wing: *Black bear*
Head: *Black*

Follow the instructions for the Polar Shrimp (page 136), but note that the body is tied in three parts. Substitute the appropriate materials.

Skunk

Like most of the steelhead patterns given, this fly is universally used throughout the North West right up to and including Alaska.

Hook: *2-6 salmon hook*
Thread: *Pre-waxed black*
Tail: *Scarlet hackle fibres*

Body: *Black chenille*
Rib: *Silver tinsel*
Hackle: *Black cock hackle*
Wing: *White polar-bear hair*
Head: *Black*

Follow the instructions for the Polar Shrimp (page 136), substituting the appropriate materials.

Skykomish Sunrise

A very popular steelhead pattern devised by George McLeod of Seattle. It is used generally as a pattern for the summer-run steelhead.

Hook: *2-12 salmon hook*
Thread: *Pre-waxed black*
Tail: *Mixed scarlet and yellow cock-hackle fibres*
Body: *Red chenille*
Rib: *Silver tinsel*
Hackle: *Mixed collar hackle of scarlet and yellow*
Wing: *White polar bear or calf tail*
Head: *Black*

Follow the instructions for the Polar Shrimp (page 136), substituting the appropriate materials.

Steelhead Caddis

This pattern is a variation of the muddler-type of fly and is used as a surface pattern for summer-running steelhead. The body of the fly is abbreviated, exposing half of the shank.

Hook: *4-12 salmon hook light wire*
Thread: *Pre-waxed black*
Body: *Either brown rabbit fur or orange fur*
Wing: *Slim slips of mottled Turkey*
Head & Collar Hackle: *Spun deer hair*

1

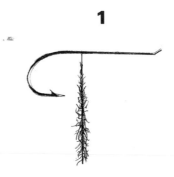

Take the tying thread half-way down the shank, and dub on the rabbit fur or the orange fur as the case maybe.

2

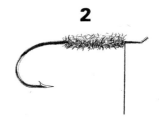

Take the fur-laden thread up the shank to form the body

3

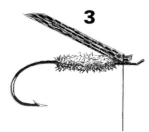

Tie in two narrow slips of mottled Turkey, placed back-to-back, on top of the hook at an angle of approximately 45 degrees.

4

Spin in the deer hair to form the head and the collar hackle. Clip the deer hair to shape and finish the fly in the usual manner.

Stillaguamish Sunrise

Another fly from the George McLeod stable, used right through the Northwest from British Columbia down to Idaho. There is little to choose between this fly and the Skykomish Sunrise.

Hook: *2-12 salmon hook*
Thread: *Pre-waxed red or black*
Tail: *Mixed red and yellow hackle fibres*
Body: *Fluorescent yellow chenille*
Rib: *Flat silver tinsel*
Hackle: *Orange throat hackle*
Wing: *White polar bear or calf tail*
Head: *Red*

Follow the instructions for the Polar Shrimp (page 136), substituting the appropriate materials.

Peter Spencer, an acknowledged expert on the Carron beat of the River Spey, works his way slowly down the noted Bothy Pool.

VI SEA-TROUT FLIES

Fiery Brown

A traditional Irish fly of long lineage, the Fiery Brown is used mainly on still waters but has many adherents among the ranks of sea-trout anglers. Michael Rogan of Ballyshannon, Co. Donegal, is closely associated with this pattern, but there are a number of different versions. The fly given here is the generally accepted pattern. It is sometimes tied with a tag of yellow floss and a tail of Golden Pheasant tippet. It is a fair representation of a sedge fished wet and can be interpreted as the hatching pupa. Fiery Brown can best be described as a deep chestnut with red inclinations.

Hook: *Down-eyed 8-12*
Thread: *Brown*
Body: *Fiery-brown seal's fur or substitute*
Rib: *Fine oval gold tinsel*
Hackle: *Dark-brown hen hackle or dyed, fiery-brown, soft-fibred cock hackle*
Wing: *Dark-bronze Mallard shoulder (as dark as possible)*
Head: *Brown*

1

Take the thread down the hook to the bend, and tie in a length of fine oval gold tinsel. Dub the seal's fur onto the tying thread.

2

Wind the fur-laden thread up the shank to form the body, and follow this with even turns of the rib.

3

Wind on the hackle. Three turns should be sufficient. Tie in and cut off any surplus hackle feather.

4

Carefully strip the good side of a dark-bronze Mallard flank feather. Select a bunch and fold or roll it, dampening it by a touch between your lips. Offer the wing to the top of the hook and, using the pinch-and-loop method, tie it on.

5

Form a neat head and complete the fly in the usual way.

Gad Fly

Anyone who has been fortunate enough to fish in the Inyanga region of the Eastern Highlands of Zimbabwe may well have met the originator of this fly, Gordon MacPherson, by the water's edge or in the Troutbeck Inn sampling a Castle Lager. He has had enormous success with this very versatile pattern. I have used it for trout and sea trout with equal success. Gordon is a flytier of extraordinarily high standard and one of the few people who can impart his knowledge to his pupils with ease, even the most intricate and difficult of patterns.

The Gad Fly is a common name for one of the biting horseflies. However, the fly depicted here has nothing to do with such creatures and is purely an attractor pattern. As can be seen, this fly is a scaled-down version of the fully dressed salmon fly used by sea-trout anglers.

Hook: *Down-eyed 8-12*
Thread: *Pre-waxed black*
Tail: *Golden Pheasant crest and a small tuft of scarlet feather fibre*
Body: *In two halves: rear yellow floss silk, front black floss silk*
Rib: *Fine silver oval tinsel*
Hackle: *Guinea Fowl hackle fibres*
Wing: *A built wing: yellow, red, and blue Goose or Swan, with a strand of green Peacock herl over this*
Cheek: *Jungle Cock or substitute*
Head: *Black*

Follow the instructions for the Silver Doctor (page 96) and substitute the appropriate materials.

Harry Tom

A famous pattern from Wales, the Harry Tom hails from the Ogwen Valley. It is a dull-looking fly but its very sobriety proves attractive to the sewin (sea trout) both by day and by night.

Hook: *Down-eyed 6-16*
Thread: *Pre-waxed black*
Tail: *Honey-dun hackle fibres*
Body: *Rabbit fur*
Rib: *Silver wire*
Hackle: *Honey dun*
Wing: *Bronze Mallard*
Head: *Black*

Follow the tying procedures for the soft-winged wet flies, such as any of the Mallard or Teal winged flies, for instance, Teal Green & Silver on page 98.

Haslam

This is one of the best-known Welsh salmon and sea-trout flies. It is very popular on such rivers as the Dovey and the Mawddach in the old county of Merioneth in the west of Wales. Many versions of this fly have been created.

Hook: *Up-eyed salmon hook 8-10*
Thread: *Pre-waxed black*
Tag: *Flat silver tinsel*
Tail: *Golden Pheasant crest*
Butt: *White wool or floss silk*
Body: *Flat silver tinsel*
Rib: *Oval silver tinsel*
Hackle: *Blue Jay or dyed blue Guinea Fowl hackle fibres*
Wing: *Hen Pheasant centre tail*
Horns: *Blue Macaw or substitute*
Head: *Black*

Note
The bright tails of the Macaw are extremely scarce, so it is now usual to substitute with blue dyed Goose or similar.

1

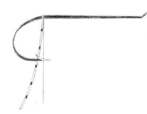

Take the thread down the shank to the bend and tie in a strip of the flat silver tinsel for the tag.

2

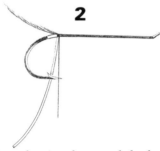

Wrap the tinsel around the hook to form the tag. Secure it and remove the surplus. Tie in a Golden Pheasant crest for the tail. At the same point tie in a length of the white wool or floss silk for the butt.

3

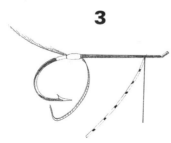

Wind on the butt material and secure and remove any excess. Tie in a strip of the oval silver tinsel at this point. Return the thread back up the shank and tie in another strip of the flat silver tinsel for the body.

4

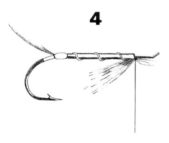

Form the body by winding the tinsel up the shank and back. Follow with the rib. Secure and cut off the excess. Tie in a bunch of blue Jay hackle fibres under the hook.

5

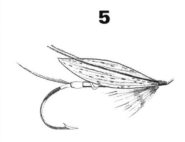

Take a strip from the left and a strip from the right side of a hen Pheasant centre tail and tie them in on top of the hook. On either side of the hook tie in a strand of blue Macaw tail or substitute, for the horns. Finish the fly with a neat head, whip finish, and varnish.

Medicine Fly

This fly, created by Hugh Falkus, is no more than a traditional Teal Blue and Silver without a tail and with a red head. Sometimes, instead of a Teal wing, bronze Mallard or Widgeon can be used for the wing feather, because it does not seem to matter to the fish. The fly was christened by Brigadier G.H.N. Wilson and is thought to be one of the best all-round seatrout flies devised by Hugh Falkus. It is very important that the fly be tied as slim as possible. Shown here are the Teal and the Bronze Mallard patterns of the Medicine Fly.

(*Above*) Teal Medicine Fly
(*Below*) Bronze Mallard Medicine Fly

Hook: *Low-water salmon hook sizes 6-10*
Thread: *Pre-waxed red*
Body: *Flat silver tinsel, the original used a silver paint*
Hackle: *Light blue*
Wing: *Teal flank (or Mallard or Widgeon)*
Head: *Red*

Tie in the same way as the Teal Green & Silver (page 98), substituting the appropriate materials.

Secret Weapon

Another highly effective Hugh Falkus fly for sea trout, this has a flying treble hook instead of a tail. It is used to catch those fish that play around with the fly and come short. Sometimes the treble is tipped with a small maggot or two, although some rivers do not allow this. It is usually fished on a sinking line.

Hook: *Down-eyed 8-10 with a 14-16 flying treble*
Thread: *Pre-waxed red*
Body: *Brown seal's fur or substitute*
Wing: *Bronze Mallard*
Hackle: *Brown cock hackle*
Head: *Red*

The nylon linkage should be approx 20lbs breaking strain so that the treble keeps rigid and does not flop down.

1

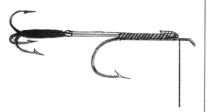

Whip a loop of nylon to the treble hook in much the same way as for the Sunk Lure (opposite). Varnish the thread whippings. Take the treble out of the vice and replace with the normal hook. Whip the nylon to the hook.

2

When the whipping on the hook is dry, tie up the Secret Weapon in the same way as any of the soft-winged wet flies (see Teal Green & Silver, page 98).

Sunk Lure

This multi-hook fly is basically a tandem version of Hugh Falkus's Medicine Fly (page 147). It is used when a large lure is required for night-time fishing for sea trout.

Hook: *Tandem rig with two down-eyed 8-10 hooks linked by nylon. They can also be tied with a long-shank hook and a low-water salmon hook in tandem. The nylon must be at least 24 lb breaking strain.*
Thread: *Pre-waxed red*
Bodies: *Flat silver tinsel*
Rib *(optional): Oval silver tinsel*
Wing: *Blue cock hackle with Peacock herl over*
Hackle: *None*
Head: *Red*

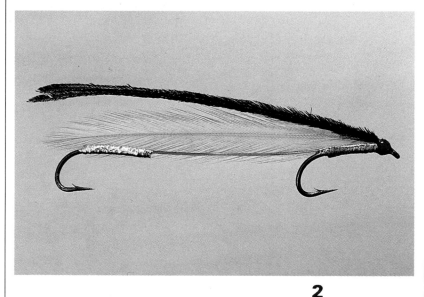

2

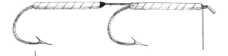

Dress the rear hook first: tie and wind on the flat silver tinsel, follow with an oval tinsel rib (if desired), tie off, and whip finish. Remove the hook from the vice and replace with the front hook. Tie a silver body on this hook, as with the rear hook.

1

Prepare the tandem linkage first. Cut a length of nylon approximately five times the length of the hook shank. Place the hook in the vice and snip off the eye with strong pliers. Now tie the nylon onto the top of the hook. When you get to the bend of the hook, fold the nylon over and take the tying thread back to the eye, covering the nylon with close turns of the thread. Whip the end and coat the whole body with varnish (some use a quick-setting adhesive) for security. Take the hook out of the vice and put the front hook in. Take the tying thread down the shank to the bend and, as with the rear hook, tie the nylon in. The upper drawing shows the configuration of the nylon for both hooks. By tying in this way the chance of the nylon pulling out is very remote. Varnish the body as in the rear hook.

3

Tie on the two blue cock hackles back-to-back in the usual way. They should extend over both hooks, but not further. Tie in two strands of Peacock herl. Finish the fly in the usual manner.

Teifi Terror

As its name suggests, this fly hails from the River Teifi in mid-Wales, famous for its run of sewin (Welsh sea trout). The original fly was not a tandem, and this form is a more recent innovation.

Hook: *Down-eyed 8-10*
Thread: *Pre-waxed black*
Tail: *Furnace cock-hackle fibres*
Body: *Black floss silk*
Rib: Oval *Gold tinsel*
Hackle: *Dark furnace*
Front Hook: *As rear hook but without tail*
Head: *Black*

1

Form a tandem rig as in the Sunk Lure pattern given on page 149.

2

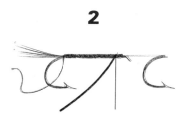

Place the rear hook in the vice and take the thread down the shank to the bend, where you tie in some furnace cock-hackle fibres for the tail. At the same point tie in a length of oval gold tinsel for the rib. Return the thread back up the shank, and there tie in a length of black floss silk.

3

Form the body by winding the floss silk down the shank and back again. Follow this with the rib. Secure and cut off any surplus material.

4

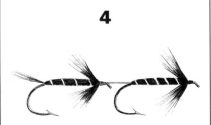

Wind on the dark furnace hackle and finish off the rear fly with a whip finish and varnish. Repeat the procedure for the front fly but leave out the tail.

VII
TUBE
FLIES

Tube flies are not, as many believe, a new phenomenon. The first tube flies were probably tied on quills not long after the turn of the century. However, it is in the last forty years that they have come into their own. The well-known tackle firm, Sharpes of Aberdeen, was one of the first companies to produce them on a commercial basis under their "Scottie" label. The advantage of a tube fly lies in the treble hook at the business end. If a single hook holds a fish, then it stands to reason that three sharp barbs will do it even better. The other feature which helped to make these tube flies popular was the fact that large heavy tubes could be used for heavy-water fishing. Furthermore, many anglers believed, and they were probably right, that large conventional flies with long shanks could well be levered out of the fish's mouth. When a salmon takes a tube fly, the hook remains in the jaw and the tube portion of the fly is sent back up the leader, preventing the leverage that might occur.

Tube flies are commercially available from ½" to 3" in brass or copper and are lined with polythene (**1**). Slightly lighter aluminium tubes are generally sold from ½" to 3" and are also polythene-lined (**2**). For lower water conditions, plastic tubes are used. These usually have an internal recess to take the eye of the treble (**3**). The brass and aluminium tubes have no such recess, but the hook can be held in the straight plane by means of a piece of valve rubber. Very small tubes, down to ¼", are sometimes used on their own, or a couple may be slipped onto the line to produce a longer fly (**4**). Amateur flytiers have constructed their own tubes from ballpoint-pen ink carriers or from medical polythene tubing. Metal tubing is also available from most model shops, but this has to be hacksawed, smoothed, and then lined with a polythene inner.

The actual dressings for tube flies are basically very simple. There are no traditionally accepted correct dressings as such. Most tubes flies tied today are left

to the imagination of the flytier and the material available. As a general rule, the conversion of a standard salmon fly to a tube-style fly follows the precept that the body remains more or less the same, while the wings are left to the discretion of the flytier, who endeavours to achieve the basic colour found in the original dressing.

Tying a tube fly

Some modern vices have a tube-fly adaptor for holding the tubes, but the same effect can be achieved by using tapered, eyeless hooks or even needles or bodkins of the correct diameter. I more often than not use the eyeless hook (figures *a* and *b*).

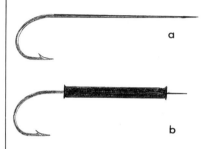

As an example, let us look at a popular pattern, the Stoat's Tail.

Stoat's Tail

Tube: *½" to 3"*
Thread: *Black*
Body: *Black floss silk*
Rib: *Oval silver tinsel*
Wing: *Black hair such as dyed squirrel or bucktail*
Head: *Black*

1

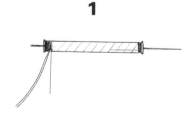

Slip the tube onto the retainer and take the thread down the tube. At the rear end, tie in a length of oval silver tinsel.

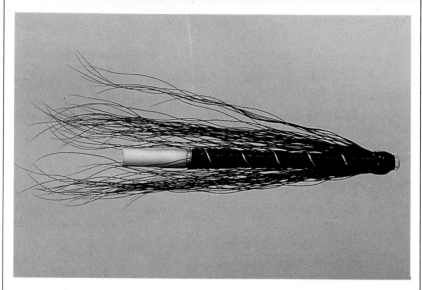

2

Return the thread back to the front end of the tube and there tie in a length of black floss silk for the body. Be generous with the length of floss silk – it is remarkable how much silk is required to cover the shank.

3

Wind the black silk thread down the tube and back again to form a smooth body. Tie off and cut away any surplus silk.

4

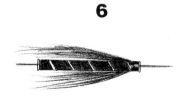

Take the oval silver ribbing tinsel back along the tube in neat turns, tie off, and remove any surplus tinsel. (If so desired, a few turns of the ribbing tinsel can be wound around the rear of the tube to form a tag. This can be done on all tube-fly patterns).

5

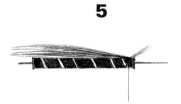

Select a bunch of black hair to suit the size of the tube. The hair must be longer than the tube itself.

6

Turn the tube around on its retainer and tie in another bunch of black hair. Trim any hair fibres that stick out beyond the head (I use a razor blade for this). Whip finish and varnish in the usual way.

7

Other tube patterns may call for a hackle. This is applied in bunches around the head of the tube.

8

Sometimes a pattern may require a body hackle as well as a wing. This is tied by the tip at the rear end and then palmered up the tube after the body has been formed. It is then followed by the rib.

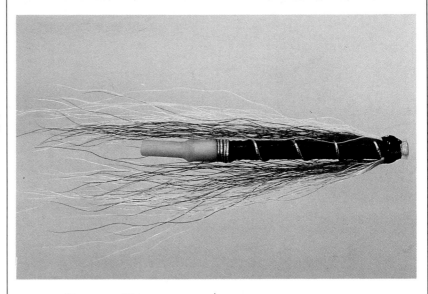

Garry Dog

This pattern, tied either on a conventional hook or on a tube, is perhaps one of the best-known salmon hairwing flies. The fly was devised by John Wright, son of the famous flytier James Wright, of Sprouston, Scotland. The original hair for the fly was taken from John Wright's Golden Retriever, hence the name. The alternative name is Yellow Dog.

Tube: *All types 1" to 3"*
Thread: *Pre-waxed black*
Body: *Black floss silk*
Rib: *Oval gold tinsel*
Wing: *Yellow and scarlet squirrel or bucktail*
Hackle: *Blue-dyed Guinea Fowl (optional on the tube fly)*
Head: *Black varnish*

Follow the instructions for the Stoat's Tail (opposite) and substitute the appropriate materials.

Silver Doctor

Others in the "Doctor" series include the Blue Doctor and the Black Doctor. To produce these in the tube-fly mode, just alter the body dressing, using blue floss silk for the Blue Doctor and black floss silk for the Black Doctor. The wing is the same for all three flies.

Tube: *All types ½" to 2"*
Thread: *Pre-waxed red*
Body: *Flat silver tinsel*
Rib: *Oval silver tinsel*
Wing: *Yellow hair with blue hair over*
Head: *Red*

This is tied in the same way as for the Stoat's Tail (opposite) but with the appropriate materials.

Silver Stoat (Mini Tube)

This pattern is extremely effective for both salmon and sea trout. The flies depicted are tied down to ¼" tubes. More than one tube can be slipped onto the line to increase the size of the fly.

Tube: *Plastic ¼" to 1"*
Thread: *Pre-waxed black*
Body: *Flat silver tinsel*
Rib (optional): *Fine silver wire*
Wing: *Black squirrel (though the tube is small enough to use actual stoat's tail)*
Head: *Black*

Jock Scott

Thread: *Pre-waxed black*
Body: *Rear half in orange, front half in black floss silk*
Rib: *Oval silver tinsel*
Wing: *Mixed yellow, red, and blue hair*
Head: *Black*

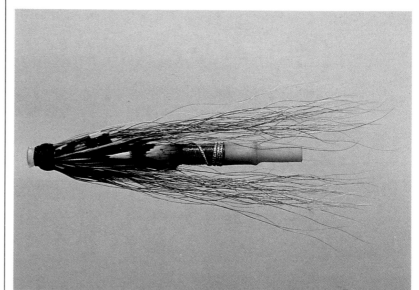

Willie Gunn

This fly has a brilliant record for spring salmon in the Scottish rivers Brora and Helmsdale. It was designed by Rob Wilson in the late 1960s.

Tube: *All types 1" to 3"*
Thread: *Pre-waxed black*
Body: *Black floss silk*
Rib: *Oval gold tinsel*
Wing: *Mixed yellow and orange red with black squirrel or bucktail over*
Head: *Black*

VIII
WADDINGTONS

Another method of using the treble hook is not on a tube but on a separate metal shank. Richard Waddington, author of the book *Salmon Fishing,* struck upon the idea. The shanks shown here are all doubles, although a single-shank Waddington is still available.

1

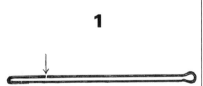

Waddingtons are tied in much the same way as are tube flies, but the treble must be slipped onto the shank first. Take a small piece of bicycle-valve rubber and push it over the eye of the treble. Slip the treble onto the shank and take the tying thread down the shank to secure the treble. (I always coat the tying thread with varnish at this stage.) Peel the valve rubber back over the eye of the treble and the end of the Waddington shank.

2

The treble is now on the same plane as the shank and will not hang down and get in the way of the winging hair. Place the shank in the vice at the point where the valve rubber ends. Then treat the pattern exactly as for the tube fly just given (page 152).

Black & Yellow

Thread: *Pre-waxed black*
Body: *Black floss silk*
Rib: *Oval gold tinsel*
Wing: *Mixed yellow and black squirrel or bucktail*
Head: *Black*

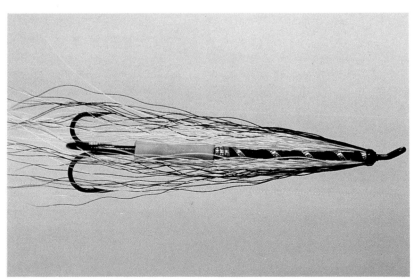

Garry Dog

This pattern is exactly the same as the Garry Dog tube fly in both materials and manner of tying (page 153).

Silver Doctor

This pattern is exactly the same as the Silver Doctor tube fly in both materials and manner of tying (page 153).

Stoat's Tail

This pattern is exactly the same as the Stoat's Tail tube fly in both materials and manner of tying (page 152).

FURTHER READING

Bates, Joseph D., Jr. *The Art of the Atlantic Salmon Fly.* David R. Godine, Boston, 1987.

Brooks, Charles E. *Nymph Fishing for Larger Trout.* Crown Publishers, New York, 1976.

Clarke, Brian. *The Pursuit of Stillwater Trout.* A & C Black, London, 1975.

Clarke, Brian *and* Goddard, John. *The Trout & the Fly.* Ernest Benn, London, 1980.

Collyer, David. *Fly Dressing I.* David & Charles, Newton Abbot, 1975.
Fly Dressing II. David & Charles, Newton Abbot, 1981.

Dawes, Mike. *The Flytier's Manual.* William Collins & Sons, London and Stoeger, South Hackensack, N.J., 1985.

Dick, Lenox. *The Art & Science of Fly Fishing.* Lyle Stuart, Secausus, N.J., 1977.

Dunham, Judith. *The Art of the Trout Fly.* Chronicle Books, San Francisco, 1988.

Halford, F.M. *Floating Flies and How to Dress Them.* Sampson Low, London, 1886.

Lane, Joscelyn. *Lake and Loch Fishing.* Seely Service, London, 1954.

Lee, Art. *Fishing: Dry Flies for Trout on Rivers & Streams.* Atheneum, New York, 1983.

Leiser, Eric. *Book of Fly Patterns.* Knopf, New York, 1987.

Leiser, Eric *and* Boyle, Robert H. *Stoneflies for the Angler.* Knopf. New York, 1982.

Malone, E.J. *Irish Trout & Salmon Flies.* Colin Smythe, London, 1984.

Martin, Darrel. *Flytying Methods.* Nick Lyons Books, New York, 1987.

Kingsmill Moore, T.C. *A Man May Fish.* Herbert Jenkins, London 1960.

Rolt, H.A. *Fishing in South Country Streams.* Sampson Low, London, 1901.

Schwiebert, Ernest G., Jr. *Matching the Hatch.* Stoeger, South Hackensack, N.J.

Veniard, John *Lake and Reservoir Flies.* A & C Black, London, 1970.

Wright, Leonard M., Jr. *Fishing the Dry Fly as a Living Insect.* Nick Lyons Books, New York, 1988.

INDEX

Note

For each fly pattern described in the book, a hook size and type is given. The author's preference after many years' experience is the Kamasan hook, and for those who want to know the exact hook number used, we give it here immediately after the fly's name.

Patterns that are shown in photographs are siven in bold, as are the page numbers on which the photographs are to be found.

INDEX